YORK NOTES

TOP GIRLS

CARYL CHURCHILL

NOTES BY KATE DORNEY

Longman

York Press

The right of Kate Dorney to be identified as Author
of this Work has been asserted by her in accordance
with the Copyright, Designs and Patents Act 1988

YORK PRESS
322 Old Brompton Road, London SW5 9JH

PEARSON EDUCATION LIMITED
Edinburgh Gate, Harlow,
Essex CM20 2JE, United Kingdom
Associated companies, branches and representatives throughout the world

Quotations from *Top Girls* by Caryl Churchill are from the
Methuen Student Edition published by Methuen Drama,
an imprint of A & C Black Publishers (2005)

First published 2008
Second impression 2009

ISBN 978–1–4058–9623–8

Phototypeset by Chat Noir Design, France
Printed in China

CONTENTS

PART FOUR
CRITICAL PERSPECTIVES

PART FIVE
BACKGROUND

PART ONE

INTRODUCTION

STUDYING PLAYS

Reading plays and exploring them critically can be approached in a number of ways, but when reading the text for the first time it is a good idea to consider some, or all, of the following:

- **Format and style**: how do plays differ from other genres of text? How are scenes or acts used to reveal information, and how do the characters convey their emotions?

- **The writer's perspective**: consider what the writer has to say, how he or she presents a particular view of people, the world, society, ideas, issues, etc. Are, or were, these views controversial?

- **Shape and structure**: explore the relationship between scenes and acts, plots and sub-plots, and how the action of the play develops – the moments of revelation and reflection, openings and endings, conflicts and resolutions.

- **Choice of language**: does the writer choose to write formally or informally? Does he or she use different registers for characters or groups, vary the sound and style, or employ verse, prose and other language features such as **imagery** and **dialect**?

- **The play in performance**: how do you imagine the play being performed? What contribution might set design and the actors' voices and movements make?

- **Links and connections**: what other texts does this play remind you of? Can you see connections between its **narrative**, main characters and ideas and those of other texts you have studied? Is the play part of a literary movement or tradition?

- **Your perspective and that of others**: what are your feelings about the play? Can you relate to the characters, themes and ideas? What do others say about the play – for example, critics, other writers, actors and directors?

These York Notes offer an introduction to *Top Girls* and cannot substitute for close reading of the text and the study of secondary sources.

CHECK THE BOOK

Linda Fitzsimmons's *File on Churchill* (1989) is an extremely useful reference work outlining all of Churchill's plays (up to *Fugue*), and reproducing reviews and other criticism.

READING *TOP GIRLS*

READING *TOP GIRLS*

CONTEXT

Social problem plays were written at the beginning of the nineteenth century and explored serious social themes like the rights of women, marriage and the treatment of the poor. The plays were usually **well made** – structured to reveal information at strategic points and make sure any dilemma was resolved by the end of the play – which explains Taylor's 'until we find out all there is to know'.

CHECK THE BOOK

Arthur Wing Pinero (1855–1934) was an actor turned playwright who wrote farces and social dramas. His most famous works are *The Second Mrs Tanquerary* (social drama) and *Trelawney of the Wells* (comedy).

Top Girls was first performed at the Royal Court Theatre in London on 28 August 1982, directed by Max Stafford-Clark. Churchill was already an established writer for radio, stage and television when *Top Girls* was produced and the play revisits subjects that had preoccupied her throughout the 1970s as well as introducing others she would explore in subsequent plays. Most prominently these subjects include gender and sexuality, capitalism and changing social relations in Britain. Churchill, Stafford-Clark and the Royal Court Theatre all had a reputation for producing work that examined contemporary issues, often in challenging and confrontational ways. The play's critical reception – which consists of reviews of professional productions, reflections on the business of making the play by actors, directors and designers and academic criticism – refers to the theatre and director almost as much and as often as it refers to the play and the playwright: a useful reminder that theatre is a collaborative business.

Top Girls was generally well received by the critics when it was first produced, although there was some confusion about its message. Some saw it as a condemnation of capitalist values (as held by Marlene and her colleagues at the Top Girls Agency); some as a feminist celebration of women's achievements; and others as a criticism of the new breed of feminists who had rejected the notion of collective action and mutual support in favour of individual achievement. The critic John Russell Taylor even regarded the play as part of the social 'problem' play tradition of the late nineteenth century and early twentieth century, commenting:

> The play proves to be a fundamentally good, old-fashioned piece with clues planted and secrets kept and revealed, climaxing in a splendidly sustained kitchen sink drama … until we find out all there is to know … it could be Pinero. (John Russell Taylor, *Plays and Players*, 350 (1982), pp. 22–3)

But we never do find out 'all there is to know'. The relationship between the sisters remains unresolved; as does the future of the younger girls, Angie, Shona and Kit – all these things are left hanging, to be decided in the 'frightening' future (Act 3, p. 87).

Top Girls examines the place of women in the world, specifically in the workplace, at the beginning of the 1980s through the character of Marlene, a woman who embodies the Thatcherite values of individual ambition at the expense of others. She rejects the socialist notion of 'from each according to his abilities, to each according to their needs' and believes that everyone makes their own luck, as she tells Joyce: 'Anyone can do anything if they've got what it takes' (Act 3, p. 6).

The first act provides the background to the role and perception of women throughout history through a dinner party in which women from different centuries and cultural traditions gather together to celebrate Marlene's promotion to 'top girl' (managing director) at the Top Girls Employment Agency. The second act shows women as workers, mothers and daughters and sketches out the challenges facing them in the 1980s. For Marlene's colleagues and the women they interview, the world of work is shifting fast and there are opportunities to be taken. For teenagers Angie and Kit, the world is changing and they are struggling to understand it. For Joyce, attempting to make ends meet doing four different jobs, the new world is much less attractive. In the third act, we are taken back to the year before Marlene's promotion when she goes to visit Joyce and Angie. We discover that Marlene is Angie's natural mother, and that Joyce adopted her, believing she might be unable to have children of her own. Joyce has literally been left behind holding the baby, caring for their ageing mother and cleaning for the rich women she despises while Marlene has pursued a career that will turn her into the kind of rich woman her sister hates. The sisters are united by their history but divided by their politics.

By introducing a cast of historical and mythical women, Act 1 provides an overview of the experiences of women throughout history and across cultures. It seems that Marlene is the latest in a long line of women, which starts with Joan (a mythical figure 'thought to have been Pope between 854-856', Note on characters), who struggled against traditional notions of femininity, and gained

CONTEXT

Margaret Thatcher was the first female British Prime Minister (from 1979 to 1990). Thatcherite policies were based on the belief that people should rely on their own ambition and ingenuity to succeed: it was intended that state welfare (housing, health and unemployment and disability benefits) should be reduced.

CHECK THE BOOK

Approaching Top Girls (1991) includes a recording of the entire BBC production directed by Max Stafford-Clark and interviews with Churchill, Stafford-Clark, Lesley Manville, Lesley Sharp, Deborah Findlay and American academics who have staged the play.

a degree of success and/or personal fulfilment. Marlene's toast reinforces this idea: 'We've all come a long way. To our courage and the way we changed our lives and our extraordinary achievements' (p. 13).

By the end of the act, the sacrifices made by each woman during their extraordinary lives raise questions about how far women really have come, and whether women's lives have improved. The following acts continue to examine this theme, depicting a range of women and their experiences of work, relationships and personal fulfilment. For Marlene and her colleagues, there is the grim possibility of turning into Louise – a woman who gave up everything for her career and still did not make it to the top – or, even worse, Mrs Kidd, who sacrificed everything for her husband and must now bear the brunt of his shame and anger at his failure to become managing director. For the younger generation, represented by Kit, Shona, Angie and Jeanine, things look bleak: there will be no help from those higher up the ladder and no one to catch them if they fall. For Joyce, Mrs Kidd and the historical characters from Act 1, a life of sacrifice bears little reward either: there are no easy answers.

Top Girls captures the burgeoning spirit of ambition and enterprise promoted by the Conservative Party under the leadership of Margaret Thatcher. Churchill's description of the play's genesis emphasises the impact Thatcher had: 'In 1979 I started thinking about a play that would have a lot of women characters doing various jobs and of course the same year Thatcher got in for the first time' (Churchill, *Plays: 2* (1990), p. i).

Margaret Thatcher was dynamic and ambitious: she revelled in the nickname 'the Iron Lady' and was the antithesis of the stereotypes of the left-wing, liberal earth mother or strident feminist in dungarees and boots as conveyed by the media in the 1970s and 1980s. For Churchill and many others, it was clear that Thatcher 'wasn't a sister' and that she was not interested in promoting the rights and welfare of women. To them, she seemed more interested in assisting the individual to achieve wealth and in playing politics in accordance with the male tradition. (In the satirical TV puppet show *Spitting Image* she was always dressed in a pinstripe suit like a man.) Like Marlene, she could have worn trousers to work, but she chose not to: she combined a feminine appearance with masculine values.

Although women's ability to determine their future is a relatively recent concept, and the extent of that freedom is still debated by feminists, studies of their lives and behaviour have always formed a large part of literature. Patient Griselda, one of the characters in *Top Girls*, is a case in point. She is the subject of poems by Petrarch, one of Boccaccio's tales in the *Decameron*, and Chaucer's 'Clerk's Tale' from *The Canterbury Tales*. All these texts celebrate the qualities that make her an ideal wife: beauty, humility, obedience and patience. Her complicity in her own abuse, however, makes her an unsympathetic character for the other women in Act 1 of Churchill's play. In many early plays women were either idealised or demonised; those drawn from Greek myth or Roman history, for example, tend to either idealise women (Odysseus's wife, Penelope, is praised in the same terms as Griselda), or blame them for misfortune (Helen of Troy is deemed responsible for the Trojan War and the downfall of the entire Trojan empire, and Cleopatra brings about the collapse of the Roman alliance led by three powerful men). Several of Shakespeare's plays concern themselves with the nature of women and their treatment, for example *The Taming of the Shrew* in which Katherina has to be taught obedience before she is deemed suitable to become a wife.

The perception and role of women on stage in Britain has evolved with their increased involvement in the writing and producing of theatre. Women were not allowed to perform on stage until the seventeenth century, up to then female roles were played by boys. When women first began to work as actors they were often seen as little better than prostitutes (a belief held by some right into the late nineteenth century), but such work did offer women a degree of liberation because it gave them a means of both earning a living and determining their own representation. In **Restoration comedy**, women characters are often witty, attractive (if young) and clever, manipulating older men (husbands and fathers) in order to obtain a preferred husband or a lover, rather than live a life of sexual

CHECK THE BOOK

Margaret Atwood's *The Penelopiad* (2005) is a reworking of the myth of Odysseus which focuses on his wife, Penelope, rather than on his wanderings and on her ambivalent feelings about his return. It is part of the feminist tradition of rewriting canonical narratives and repositioning the female characters at the centre of them (see **Literary background**).

CONTEXT

Aphra Behn
(1640–89) was the
first professional
English woman
playwright. Many
of her comedies
deal with the
predicament of
women being
made to marry for
money. Susannah
Centlivre
(1669–1723) began
her career as a
strolling player
and became a
prolific
playwright. Her
first dramatic
success was *The
Gamester* which
criticised
gambling. Her
plays remained
popular into the
nineteenth
century.

**CHECK
THE BOOK**

Henrik Ibsen's play
A Doll's House
(1879) details Nora
Helmer's growth
from her husband's
vivacious 'songbird'
whom he never
takes seriously into
a mature woman
who leaves him and
her children in
order to live an
independent life.

frustration with a rich and ailing old man. Some of the funniest **Restoration comedies** were also written by women. Aphra Behn's *The Rover* (1677) and Susannah Centlivre's *The Wonder, a Woman Keeps a Secret* (1707) both show young women manipulating their own destiny to get the husbands they want, rather than the husbands their fathers want them to have. These plays show very clearly the extent to which women were considered commodities to be bought, sold and traded, but they also articulate women's sexual desires and desire for self-determination.

By the nineteenth century, social drama (written by Shaw, Ibsen and Strindberg, for example) began to use the position of women to ask larger questions about society and its organisation. As W. B. Worthen notes: 'Playwrights frequently associated the political and social limitations of middle-class life with male characters and used female characters to pose subversive questions about that social order' (*The Harcourt Brace Anthology of Drama*, 2nd edn (1996), p. 570). Ibsen's *Hedda Gabler* (1890) and *A Doll's House* (1879), Strindberg's *Miss Julie* (1888), Shaw's *Major Barbara* (1907) and *Mrs Warren's Profession* (1902), and even Wilde's *A Woman of No Importance* (1893), although stylistically distinct, all challenge conventional views on the role of women in society and the limits of their personal freedom.

The dilemmas faced by the women in *Top Girls* have not disappeared, although they have receded a little. Twenty-five years after *Top Girls* was first produced some women in Britain still earn less than men (according to the most recent survey from the Equal Opportunities Commission – a government agency tasked with improving equality and human rights). The provision of childcare can be, in some cases, a luxury that parents cannot afford; there are still fewer women in positions of power (although the situation has improved since 1982); and feminism is sometimes seen as outdated and the preserve of the politically radical. *Top Girls* offers a chance to reassess the position of women and work in the twenty-first century, and, as a strikingly original piece of theatre, rewards close and careful study.

THE TEXT

NOTE ON THE TEXT

The edition used in these Notes is the 2005 Methuen Student Edition, edited by Bill Naismith.

Top Girls was first performed at the Royal Court theatre in London in August 1982. The play transferred to Joe Papp's Public Theatre in New York, winning an Obie, before returning to the Royal Court in 1983. As Churchill writes in the Production note (see Methuen Student Edition), she wrote the play in three acts but, in the original stage production, the interval was placed after Act 2, Scene 1 in order to sustain the pace of the action.

SYNOPSIS

The play begins with Marlene waiting for six dinner guests in a restaurant. The first to arrive is Isabella, followed by Nijo, Gret, Joan and, eventually, Griselda. Throughout the action, the women are served in silence by the waitress. During the course of the meal, which has been arranged to celebrate Marlene's promotion to managing director of Top Girls Employment Agency, each of the women reveals her life story. Isabella discovered her love of travel when she was sent abroad to convalesce; Nijo was mistress to a Japanese emperor and then became an itinerant nun; Joan disguised herself as a man and was made Pope; Griselda married a rich lord who took away her children as a test of her obedience; Gret led a troop of women into hell to extract revenge for all the suffering they had endured during the war with Spain.

The act ends with the women drunk and melancholy as they reflect on the ups and downs in their lives. Common to all their experiences is the memory of a period of happiness – no matter how brief – when they triumphed over the male-dominated world they lived in. This is summed up by the final words in the act: Isabella's

CHECK THE BOOK

In J. B. Priestley's *An Inspector Calls* (1945), a dinner party also dominates the whole of the first act and, like *Top Girls*, it shows us the characters revealing themselves through their conversations.

CONTEXT

The fact that all the guests except Marlene are dead would not necessarily be immediately obvious to the audience when Isabella and Nijo appear (it could be a fancy dress party for example). This first impression may have been reinforced in the first production by the fact that Nijo was played by the actress Lindsay Duncan, who is tall and blonde, and no attempt was made to disguise this. She simply wore a Japanese costume, had her hair up in a bun and was made up to resemble a Japanese noblewoman.

recollection of her final trip to 'visit the Berber Sheiks': 'I knew my return of vigour was only temporary, but how marvellous while it lasted' (Act 1, p. 29).

Act 2 begins with Marlene at work, interviewing a young woman, who is clearly not a 'top girl'. The sympathy she showed her dinner guests is conspicuously lacking from this encounter, although she is not unkind. In Scene 2, two girls (Kit and Angie) are hiding in a backyard discussing their plans for the evening, their fear of nuclear war and Angie's hatred of her mother, Joyce. Having called for them repeatedly during the scene, Joyce finally comes to fetch them in and talks to Kit while Angie tidies her room. It is clear that Angie and Joyce have a difficult relationship.

Scene 3 switches back to the Top Girls Agency where Marlene works. Her female colleagues (Win and Nell) discuss their weekend and Marlene's promotion. She arrives and they all begin work. Win and Nell are also 'top girls' and during the rest of the scene we find out about the sacrifices they have made to attain their position. The rest of the scene divides into a series of interviews: one with an older woman, one with a young woman, and in Marlene's case an interview with her colleague's wife (Mrs Kidd) and a conversation with Angie (her niece) who has run away to stay with her. Marlene is clearly displeased by Angie's appearance, although she remains, superficially at least, reasonably pleasant towards her. However, when Angie has gone, she disparages her to her colleagues, saying 'She's not going to make it' (Act 2, p. 66). The message of this act is that success is never achieved without a sacrifice, and that, often, a man's success is partly due to the sacrifices of the women in his life. Mrs Kidd's outburst summarises this point: 'It's me that bears the brunt. I'm not the one that's been promoted. I put him first every inch of the way' (Act 2, p. 58).

Act 3 takes place a year earlier than the preceding acts. Marlene has gone to visit her sister (Joyce) and Angie in her childhood home – Angie has tricked her into coming. She brings presents for both of them which only increases Angie's admiration for her. Joyce is surprised and displeased to see Marlene but tries to hide this from Angie. After Angie has gone to bed they argue, first about Angie (who we discover is Marlene's daughter), then about their mother and father, and finally about politics. Marlene's separation from her child and her family is the sacrifice she has made for success. Joyce's position is similar to that of Mrs Kidd: she sacrificed her own chance of escape in order to look after Marlene's child, raising the question, what is the good of female success if it is only at the expense of other women?

The play ends with Angie coming downstairs in the middle of a nightmare and repeating the word 'frightening', thereby summing up Churchill's fears for a future in which the pursuit of wealth is valued above humanity. Knowing this act precedes the action in the rest of the play only increases the sense of pessimism. Despite their row, we know that when Angie arrives on Marlene's doorstep she will be written off. There is no room in the Top Girls Agency for those who are 'stupid, lazy and frightened' (Act 3, p. 86); only for a 'tough bird like us' (Act 2, p. 48).

DETAILED SUMMARIES

ACT 1, PAGES 1–13

- Marlene is waiting in a restaurant at a table for six. She tells the waitress that one person will arrive late. The first guest to arrive is Isabella; she is followed by Nijo, Gret and Joan.
- Isabella and Nijo exchange stories about their travels. Joan arrives and the conversation turns to religion and relationships with men.

Marlene is hosting a dinner party in a restaurant. Her guests arrive one by one: Isabella Bird, a nineteenth-century woman traveller; Lady Nijo, a thirteenth-century courtesan to the Emperor of Japan, and then a Buddhist nun; Dull Gret, a figure from a painting by Brueghel showing a woman in armour and an apron leading a troop of women into battle against devils; and Pope Joan, a mythical

CONTEXT

Isabella Bird (1831–1904) became famous for her adventures while travelling. The daughter of a clergyman, she suffered from a spinal complaint (described in the play as a tumour on the spine) and was sent to America and Canada to convalesce in 1854. On her return she fell ill again and did not recover her health until she began travelling again at the age of 40.

figure who disguised herself as a man and was discovered only when she gave birth.

Marlene is a gracious hostess, making introductions, ensuring everyone orders their food and has enough to drink. She asks questions, establishes links between their experiences and generally tries to ensure that everyone feels part of the group. There is no attempt to explain how these women from different cultures, ages and myths are able to gather together, and the waitress's lack of astonishment at their arrival (as far as the stage directions give any indication) suggests that the play will not be in the **realist** tradition.

COMMENTARY

The fact that no explanation is given for how these different women have come to be in the restaurant affords the audience a lot of space for speculation. Is Marlene dreaming? Is the entire play set in in an afterlife and, if not, why is the waitress so blasé about their party? As well as the strange setting, members of the audience must also accustom themselves to the unusual presentation of **dialogue** in the play. Churchill attempts to make the speech ultra-realistic by orchestrating the dialogue so that more than one person talks at once and conversational threads weave backwards and forwards through the scene: a technique which depends largely on the actors' timing for its success. Audiences and readers of *Top Girls* are often baffled by the overlapping dialogue and some have found it to be extremely distracting and frustrating; it has also often been commented on by critics (see **Critical approaches: Language and style**).

This section of the act highlights the similarities and differences between women of the different cultures, religious beliefs and historical periods, represented by the assembled guests. That the play begins in a restaurant, a social space rather than a domestic one, enables the audience to learn about the characters through their behaviour in this environment. It also conveys information about Marlene's wealth: she can afford to hold a celebration for six in a restaurant, and her behaviour towards the waitress and her guests suggests that she is accustomed to doing so. From a practical point of view, the setting allows the women to focus on their storytelling rather than on cooking and serving the food. All the women, except Griselda, arrive during this part of the act and their behaviour towards each other reveals a great deal about their personalities and previous acquaintance. Marlene's familiarity with everyone suggests that she has met them before, and that perhaps they meet regularly in smaller groups: Isabella and Nijo seem to know each other as Marlene makes no attempt to introduce them, and they do not introduce themselves to each other. As the most socially sophisticated of the group, they would certainly not behave in this way if they were not already acquainted. They discuss their experiences of travel and religion, and pursue these themes further when Joan arrives.

When Gret arrives, Marlene introduces her to Nijo (without explaining her historical significance), but not to Isabella, who greets her in a familiar fashion. Gret does not acknowledge any of them verbally and throughout this section, whenever she is asked a question, she gives short, blunt replies which serve to remind us that she is a simple peasant, and so has no experience of, or capacity for, elaborate language. Her taste in food – soup, meat, potatoes and bread – is equally simple and in keeping with her background: she orders plain, stodgy food that would have kept her warm and given her lots of energy in her previous existence. Marlene shares Gret's appetite – both order steak and lots of potatoes – and also, as we discover later, her humble upbringing. Marlene makes a special effort to make Joan feel welcome: 'Do you know everyone? We were just talking about learning Latin and being clever girls. Joan was by way of an infant prodigy' (Act 1, p. 4).

One very important theme in the play addressed early on in this section is the relationship between women and male authority. Joan's arrival sparks a long discussion about religion and relationships with men among Isabella, Nijo and Joan. In the cases of Isabella and Nijo, this includes their relationships with their fathers, drawing our attention to the fact that in both eastern and western cultures, a woman went from being the property of her father to the property of her husband/lover, from the very earliest times (represented by Joan) to the early twentieth century

QUESTION

At which point do you think it becomes obvious to an audience that all the dinner guests except Marlene are dead? Is this point different depending on whether you see the play or read it?

CONTEXT

Heresy is a belief
or practice
contrary to the
teaching of the
Christian faith. It
has since been
extended to cover
any belief or
behaviour which
goes against the
established order.
Joan's remark thus
has a double
meaning.

(represented by Isabella), a structure normally described as
patriarchy. Initially Joan behaves as if she is still Pope, responding
to Nijo's story of the death of her father by declaring 'Death is the
return of all creatures to God' (Act 1, p. 4). It is only when Isabella,
who as the daughter of a vicar and wife of a doctor will have
endured many trying social occasions, tries to change the subject
by saying, 'I knew coming to dinner with a pope we should keep
off religion' (Act 1, p. 6) that Joan relaxes enough to tell her, 'I
always enjoy a theological argument. But I won't try to convert
you, I'm not a missionary. Anyway I'm a heresy myself' (Act 1,
p. 6). Joan's comment communicates two important points. First,
that she is aware of her identity as a cultural construct – a legend
within the Catholic Church. As a 'heresy', her teachings would have
been banned by the Catholic Church, and anyone continuing to
believe in her, or that she had existed, would have been punished.
Second, because she lived her life as a man, Joan has forgotten that
women were not allowed the pleasure of enjoying an intellectual
debate on religion or any other subject during her own time.
Indeed, of all the women present, only Marlene, and possibly
Isabella, will have had the opportunity to disagree with men
publicly.

As we might expect, Marlene, a product of late-twentieth-century
British society, is much more outspoken than Isabella, whose
behaviour is still conditioned by Victorian social conventions.
Marlene's twentieth-century astonishment at the achievements of
her guests, and at their attitudes to their treatment by a
patriarchal society, highlights the obstacles the women have
overcome in the course of history and the freedoms that her own
generation takes for granted. However, throughout the meal, the
women are served in silence by the waitress, a silence which serves
as a **counterpoint** to their constant overlapping talk. She is invisible
to them except when she is fulfilling their desires – a situation that
many of the guests have found themselves in their dealings with
men. This raises the issue of women not always being supportive
of each other (as the guests have been), and also the idea of them
oppressing other women. This device serves to suggest that
not all women in the twentieth century enjoy the same freedoms as
Marlene.

QUESTION

What do you think
might be gained or
lost by preserving
the overlapping
structure of the
dialogue in
performance?

GLOSSARY

1	Frascati an Italian white wine
	Tobermory small town on the coast of the Scottish island of Mull
	saki Japanese alcoholic drink made from fermented rice
2	my own pet an affectionate phrase the character of Isabella uses about her sister Hennie; it is a direct quotation from Bird's letters to her sister
3	the metaphysical poets a group of seventeenth-century poets, including John Donne, George Herbert (both clergymen) and Andrew Marvell, whose work explored the relationship of humankind to God; the relationship between the mind and the body (hence 'metaphysical'); and relationships between men and women
	hymnology the way in which hymns are composed, and/or the study of hymns
4	infant prodigy an exceptionally gifted child, who quickly masters a skill, or develops an innate talent
	John the Scot thirteenth-century philosopher, John Duns 'Scotus'. Scotus is Latin for Scot
6	Mahayana sutras stories from the Mahayana school of Buddhist literature
8	Sandwich Isles Hawaiian islands in the North Pacific Ocean
9	Mr Nugent James Nugent, also known as Rocky Mountain Jim, lived in Estes Park in the Rocky Mountains. As well as tending cattle and trapping animals he served as a guide to visitors to the Rocky Mountains and it was in this capacity that Isabella met him
10	St Augustine a Christian saint (354–430), also a scholar and exponent of Neo-Platonism
	Denys the Areopagite, the pseudo Denys Joan is presumably referring to Dionysus the Areopagite who preached that we can only describe what God is not, rather than what he is. Areopagus was the name of the supreme council of Ancient Athens and the place where the council met
11	erysipelas a bacterial infection which produces swelling and reddening of the skin
	anaemia a lack of iron in the blood which makes the sufferer weak

continued

CONTEXT

'Neo-Platonic Ideas' (p. 10) – also known as the Platonic forms – derived from Plato's writings. Essentially the idea is that for every representation of something on Earth, be it a chair, a painting or a quality like goodness or beauty, there is an ideal form of that object or quality existing beyond our human knowledge. So Joan disagrees with the idea that God is the ideal form of humankind.

| 12 | **Jaeger flannel** a sturdy tweed cloth, manufactured by Jaeger |
| 13 | **muleteers** people employed to lead the mules carrying luggage and provisions on expeditions |

ACT 1, PAGES 13–19

- The group toasts Marlene's promotion to managing director of Top Girls Employment Agency.
- Marlene's toast prompts Isabella and Nijo to remember moments when they were especially courageous.
- Joan describes her experiences as Pope up to and including the birth of her baby and her execution.
- Nijo remembers her own experiences of childbirth and children.

CONTEXT

Judith Butler's *Gender Trouble* (1990) expands on the idea that gender is created rather than inherent. She suggests that men and women learn to *perform* their gender by continually repeating certain types of behaviour, e.g. wearing make-up.

This short section points up further common ground between the women: their courage in difficult situations and their experiences of childbirth. Marlene's acknowledgement of the courage it takes to break with conventions leads Isabella and Nijo to recount specific examples of their own bravery. Joan's story puts their hardships into perspective. Not only did she suffer the mental anguish of reconciling her faith with her existence as Pope, she describes how she and her child were brutally murdered when her gender was discovered. The conclusion of Joan's story is the focus of this section and alters the mood of the party significantly, aided by the fact that the women are becoming progressively more drunk. The themes of motherhood and suffering discussed here prepare the audience for the arrival of Griselda, the final guest.

COMMENTARY

Marlene's toast acts as the catalyst for this next section of the meal: 'We've all come a long way. To our courage and the way we changed our lives and our extraordinary achievements' (Act 1, p. 13). Her use of 'we' and 'our' is significant here. It shows that Marlene considers herself as the latest in a long line of women who have struggled against traditional notions of femininity, and gained a degree of success and/or personal fulfilment. It also shows her determination to celebrate the achievements of women who have been largely forgotten by history. The specific instances of Isabella and Nijo offer further insights into their personalities. For Isabella, it was 'crossing a mountain pass at seven thousand feet', and for Nijo, spending 'four months lying alone at an inn' (Act 1, p. 13). Isabella prides herself on overcoming her physical impairments, while Nijo's victory is in spending so much time without anyone ministering to her. It is clear that it was always difficult for these two to exist without a network of loving support from their families and lovers, and that they have been conditioned to think of themselves, and their bodies, as weak. This explains their pride in recalling the occasions on which they managed without these things.

Again, Joan's experiences act as a foil to those of the other guests. Nijo's body was the thing that made her powerful and she looked after it accordingly. Isabella's body was the thing that held her back, and she defied her bad health in order to travel. Joan is almost entirely ignorant about her own body. The Catholic Church taught that the body was merely the vessel of the spirit and that the holy should place the cultivation of the mind above the body. This, in addition to having always lived and thought of herself as a man, means that Joan's ignorance of her own body leads to her downfall. Instead of managing her pregnancy as skilfully as Nijo did with her first child (Act 1, p. 16), she tries to ignore it, with disastrous consequences. This emphasises another of the contrasts between them: Joan's uncompromising attitude – born of her religious convictions and experiences living as a powerful man – ends in her death; as a woman, Nijo became adept at exploiting the allowances accorded to someone of her gender and status. From an early age she learns to use her femininity to her advantage, recognising that it was the only power she had. Her throwaway remark about her baby – 'It was only a girl but I was sorry to lose it' (Act 1, p. 16) – underscores the low regard for women in her society. This is compounded by the revelation that her daughter would share her destiny: 'She was being brought up very carefully so she could be sent to the palace like I was' (Act 1, p.18).

 CHECK THE BOOK
The trips Isabella describes in the play to the Sandwich Isles (Hawaii), Australia, America, Japan and Morocco are all described in her published works. A shortened version of her time with Rocky Mountain Jim, taken from her 1879 book *A Lady's Life in the Rocky Mountains*, has been reissued, entitled *Adventures in the Rocky Mountains* (2007).

Joan's story changes the mood of the party. What begins as a triumph, with a woman wielding the highest form of power on earth – accepting the allegiance of the King of England and consecrating bishops – ends in her being stoned to death when she gives birth (pp. 14, 17). The stage directions dictate the swiftness with which the mood changes:

JOAN:	Far away I heard people screaming, 'The Pope is ill, the Pope is dying.' And the baby just slid out into the road.*
MARLENE.	The cardinals / won't have known where to put themselves.
NIJO.	Oh dear, Joan, what a thing to do! In the street!
ISABELLA.	*How embarrassing.
GRET.	In a field, yah.

They are laughing.

JOAN.	One of the cardinals said, 'The Antichrist!' and fell over in a faint.

They all laugh.

MARLENE.	So what did they do? They weren't best pleased.
JOAN.	They took me by the feet and dragged me out of town and stoned me to death.

They stop laughing.

(Act 1, p. 17)

The mood then lightens again as they consider the ridiculousness of the pierced chair used in the Vatican to establish that all future Popes are really men (Act 1, p. 19). Within the world of the play Joan's tenure as Pope is represented as having changed the traditions of the Catholic Church, even if she attained it at the expense of her life. The absurdity of making God's representative on earth sit in a pierced chair so that other holy men can crawl underneath and check his gender is used by Churchill to undermine the solemnity of the office and thus the power wielded by men.

CONTEXT

Catholicism and Protestantism, each a branch of the Christian faith, are distinguished from one another chiefly by their beliefs about Communion – the point in a Christian service when worshippers remember Christ's actions at the Last Supper (the meal with his disciples before his crucifixion) when he broke bread and poured wine. Catholics believe that the wine and wafer they eat and drink in memory of this turns into the body and blood of Christ – known as the theory of transub-stantiation. Protestants believe that the process is **symbolic**.

GLOSSARY

14	**consecrate** make holy or sacred
16	**Rogation Day** one of the three days before Ascension when the litany of the saints is chanted. Ascension Day marks Jesus Christ's ascension into heaven forty days after he was resurrected
19	**laird** the Scottish term for a landowner of a large estate. Lairds, like squires and marquises, usually held a position of power in the local community

ACT 1, PAGES 19–29

- Griselda arrives and is introduced by Marlene. She recounts the story of her marriage to Walter and the tests he subjected her to.
- Her unquestioning obedience in the face of Walter's cruelty horrifies Marlene and reminds Nijo of her act of defiance. Griselda begins to question Walter's actions.
- Gret tells her story.
- Isabella recalls her last triumph: visiting the Emperor of Morocco.

Griselda's arrival has been anticipated since the beginning of Act 1 when Marlene tells Isabella and Nijo that she will be late. By the time she arrives, the other guests are '*quite drunk*' and Marlene is anxious to get her to tell the story of her 'extraordinary marriage' (Act 1, pp. 19, 20). Griselda does so, with many promptings from Marlene, and many interruptions from Isabella and Nijo. When she was 15, she was selected by Walter, the local Marquis, to be his bride, on the condition that she '*must always obey him in everything*' (Act 1, p. 21). She agrees: women always have to obey men anyway, and she would rather obey a Marquis than '*a boy from the village*' (Act 1, p. 21). Throughout their marriage he tests her obedience, first by taking away her children, then by telling her he will marry another woman and she must help with the wedding arrangements. Her reward for this obedience is to be reunited with

CONTEXT

Patient Griselda, as Marlene tells us, first appears in Boccacio's *Decameron*, then Petrarch's sonnets, and then in 'The Clerk's Tale' in Chaucer's *Canterbury Tales*. All tell the story exactly as Griselda tells the assembled women; the variety is in their description of her beauty, humility and sweet nature.

her children and with Walter. (His new bride turns out to be her daughter, and the whole wedding is just an elaborate ploy to test her.) According to Griselda they all live happily ever after once she has proved herself.

All the guests except Nijo are shocked by Walter's cruelty and Griselda's defence of him. Even Nijo is reminded of an occasion on which the Emperor abused his powers and she and the other ladies of the court planned their revenge: 'I beat him till he cried out' (Act 1, p. 27). In the face of their protests, Griselda begins to have second thoughts (Act 1, p. 27). Joan is reciting Latin when Gret suddenly launches into her story of her journey to hell to fight the devils who she thought were responsible for all the misery inflicted on her village. Her story ends as suddenly as it begins, Joan resumes her recital and Isabella tells the story of her last trip to Morocco.

COMMENTARY

This section of the play builds on the themes explored throughout Act 1: the relationship between women and male authority (and the assumption of female obedience implicit within that) and the role of motherhood. Griselda's tale combines many of the elements expressed in the other women's stories. Like Gret, she was born a peasant; and, like Njio, she was selected by a powerful man to become his companion and she submitted to him in everything. In fact, so exemplary is Griselda's behaviour that it has made her famous; so much so that, as Marlene points out, men have enshrined her in literature (Act 1, p. 20). For Marlene, who is used to pleasing herself, has worked hard to attain her independence and now denies herself nothing, Griselda's patience is a source of frustration and astonishment. Even Griselda's entrance emphasises her meekness. She slips in when everyone else is laughing without greeting anybody and so no one realises that she has arrived for a few minutes. She refuses Marlene's offer of food, 'No, no, don't bother', and only succumbs once she realises everyone else is having dessert (Act 1, p. 20). Even then she asks only for cheese and biscuits, a plain dish, while Marlene asks for 'profiteroles because they're disgusting' (Act 1, p. 20). In this exchange, Marlene demonstrates her independence from men in another way: by showing her disregard for the fashion for slim women: 'We're having pudding, I am, and getting nice and fat' (Act 1, p. 20). Having an independent income means that Marlene has not had to trade on her attractiveness to men in the same way that Nijo (and possibly Griselda) has. Marlene makes her disapproval of Walter clear from the beginning; the other women are much more polite and cautious, aware by this point in the evening that stories can take an unexpected turn (as Joan's did).

Griselda's passive acceptance of her treatment prompts Nijo to recall 'something that made me angry': not the physical abuse she endured every year at the Full Moon Ceremony, but the occasion on which the Emperor breached etiquette by allowing his attendants to beat the court ladies (Act 1, p. 26). It is typical of Nijo's character that her overriding concern is the injury to her pride rather than to her body, but what is surprising is the decision made by her and the other court ladies to take revenge. The nature of the Full Moon Ceremony itself is another example of the low regard women were held in. As they all contemplate Nijo's and Griselda's stories Joan begins to recite a passage from Lucretius which advises withdrawal from the world and detachment from the sufferings of others. In view of the stories of suffering which have unfolded during this act, it is easy to see why Joan might long for solitude and contemplation.

> **CONTEXT**
>
> It is not clear which ceremony Nijo is referring to when she names the Full Moon Ceremony. The Buddhist new year is celebrated on the first full moon day in January and Buddha Day (celebrating the birth, death and enlightenment of Buddha) takes place on the first full moon day in May. However, the Japanese do not follow the lunar calendar as other Buddhist countries do so it is difficult to be sure whether this is a real ceremony or an invented one.

When Gret begins her story it is clear that she has been spurred into speech by the various tales of cruelty and suffering, in the same way as she was spurred into battle against the devils. She uses very simple and direct language – a reflection of her status as a peasant – which contrives to make the account more moving because it leaves more to the imagination. Her story is also very short, despite being even more fantastic than those of the other women – perhaps reminding the audience that a picture (which is where she originates) is worth a thousand words. Like Marlene, Gret is very straightforward in her account, and makes no attempt to excuse the actions of her oppressors (the Spanish) as the other women have done: 'We'd all had family killed. My big son die on a wheel. Birds eat him. My baby, a soldier run her through with a sword. I'd had enough, I was mad' (Act 1, p. 28).

She does not reflect on her actions at all, but exudes a grim satisfaction at having given 'them devils such a beating' (Act 1, p. 29). As Gret finishes her story, Joan resumes her recitation, and Isabella, who spurned a life of quiet contemplation for a life of action, recounts her final adventure: visiting the Emperor of Morocco. She alluded to this visit right at the beginning of the act, and gets to finish her story only at this point because of all the interruptions from the other guests. Her final words, and the final lines of the act, sum up the experiences of all the women and their attempts to resist the weight of history, convention and society: 'how marvellous while it lasted' (Act 1, p. 29). These sentiments could leave the audience confused about how they should feel at this point. Isabella's story is one of triumph over adversity, as is Gret's, but the visual **counterpoint** to her words conveys an **ironic** disjunction: Nijo *'laughing and crying'* and Joan *'being sick'* while Marlene drinks Isabella's brandy (Act 1, p. 29).

CONTEXT

The passage Joan quotes is from the beginning of Book 2 of *De rerum natura* which praises philosophy as a retreat from life.

GLOSSARY

20	**marquis** a high-ranking nobleman
27–8	**Suave, mari magno … splendorem purpureai** How pleasant it is, when the winds are stirring up the waters of a swollen sea, to watch another's perils from the shore: not because his troubles are a source of delight or joy, but because it is pleasing to recognise that one is free from troubles one's self.

It is also pleasing to witness battle being waged across a plane when one is out of that danger. But nothing is more delightful than to occupy the calm of an ivory tower which is built on the teachings of wise men. From there one can look down on others as they roam about seeking a path through life, as they strive to be wise, to surpass each other's reputation, struggling day and night to reach the top with their wealth and power.

What miserable minds they have. How blind their hearts are to waste their short span in darkness, in danger. They cannot see that all nature requires is for life to be lived free of physical pain, so the mind, free from worries, can be delighted.

ACT 2, SCENE 1

- This scene takes place in the Top Girls Employment Agency.
- Marlene is interviewing a young woman, Jeanine, who wants to find a better, more glamorous, job.

We find Marlene at the start of an interview with a new client (Jeanine) looking through her CV. She is brisk and businesslike, asking lots of questions to try and establish what kind of person Jeanine is and how serious she is about her career. Jeanine works in a small business where there is no room for promotion, she wants more money and more opportunities to develop and so she has come to the Agency to find a new job. She is hoping for a more glamorous profession, but has not realised that this will inevitably be a more competitive environment for which she has neither the skills nor the drive. Marlene tries to persuade her to be realistic, and also to think of her career as a long-term project – something Jeanine is reluctant to do. Having established Jeanine's limitations Marlene advises her to try for the posts she has on offer in a lampshade or knitwear factory.

COMMENTARY

This is a very short scene which shows Marlene at work and initiates the audience into the realities of women in the workplace in the early 1980s. Jeanine is ambitious, but in an unfocused and non-strategic way. When Marlene asks, 'So you want a job with better prospects?' (Act 2, p. 30), her immediate response is that she wants a 'change'. Only Marlene's continued probing makes her express exactly what she wants: more money and to work in a more exciting field (advertising). Marlene's pragmatism is completely at odds with this hazy sense of ambition (Jeanine is not even clear that she wants a long-term job) and although she is keen to offer her advice, it is also clear that she is not prepared to spend a lot of time on her. The constant stream of questions pushes the scene forward at a rapid pace and Marlene's businesslike conclusion to the meeting makes it clear that she does not suffer fools gladly – and certainly does not take clients on out of a sense of charity:

 CHECK THE BOOK

Alison Pearson's *I Don't Know How She Does It* (2003) recounts the struggles of a successful banker trying to juggle her career with being a 'super' wife and mother.

Now Jeanine I want you to get one of these jobs, all right? If I send you that means I'm putting myself on the line for you. Your presentation's OK, you look fine, just be confident and go in there convinced that this is the best job for you and you're the best person for the job. (Act 2, p. 33)

Jeanine does not appear to have what it takes to become a 'top girl' (no long-term plan, no readiness to make sacrifices and no sense of competition). In an age where the notion of 'having it all' – a phrase coined to describe the ambition ascribed to women in the 1990s to have a successful career, relationship and a family – had yet to be conceived, unless they were very lucky, or very wealthy, women faced a clear choice between family and career. Jeanine knows that she wants a better and more exciting life, but her indecisiveness – replying 'I might do' when Marlene questions whether or not she wants a long-term job – suggests that if her husband can provide this for her, then she might be happy to forgo her career (Act 2, p. 31). Given the conditions in which many women worked at the time, her position is entirely understandable. Marlene advises her not to mention her impending marriage as she will be perceived as a risk to the firm – potential employers might believe that women who get married often leave to have families, taking their expertise with them and putting the firm to the trouble and expense of recruiting someone new and paying for their maternity leave and cover. This is a salutary reminder that despite the Sex Discrimination Act of 1975, the status of women in the workplace was far from equal at the time this play was written.

 CHECK THE FILM

How to Get Ahead in Advertising (1989) is a satirical look at the advertising industry. An advertising executive working on a cream to treat boils grows a talking boil which pronounces advertising slogans and eventually takes him over.

Jeanine's desire for a career in advertising or marketing reflects the preoccupations of the time. The 1980s were the decade in which advertising and marketing became 'sexy'. This was seen as a sector in which creative people were well rewarded for thinking up 'witty' or 'abstract' advertising slogans. These adverts reflected the fact that there were more people with higher disposable incomes to spend on new products, such as Perrier mineral water, which was advertised through a series of puns on 'eau' (the French word for water). This explains Marlene's dry response when Jeanine says she has thought of working in advertising, 'People often do think advertising' (Act 1, p. 31), implying that lots of people think they could work in that field, but very few will get the chance to do so.

> ### GLOSSARY
>
> 30   **Os and As** Ordinary Level and Advanced Level Certificates, commonly known as O Levels and A Levels. The examinations were generally taken at 16 and 18 respectively in England; O Levels were replaced in 1987 by GCSEs
>
> **Speeds, not brilliant** a reference to words per minute typed or transcribed into shorthand

ACT 2, SCENE 2

- The scene takes places in Joyce's backyard and begins with Joyce calling for Angie (aged 16) who is sitting in a shelter with Kit (aged 12).
- Angie ignores Joyce's calls and she and Kit discuss going to the cinema.
- Angie tries to scare Kit by telling her stories about ghosts and poltergeists. It doesn't work and the girls quarrel.
- Joyce calls again, but they ignore her. Angie talks about running away to live with her aunt in London.
- Joyce comes out to fetch the girls in. Kit and Joyce talk about Angie and the future.

The scene has shifted from Marlene's office to the backyard of a house in East Anglia. Kit, who is 12, and Angie, who is 16, are hiding from Angie's mum, Joyce, in a shelter they have made from junk. Angie is brooding on her hatred of Joyce, and Kit's suggestion that they go to the cinema to see *The Exterminator* (a violent film) serves to reinforce her anger, reminding her that she is dependent on her mother for money and permission to go. She tries to bully Kit, telling her that she looks too young to get into an X-rated film, and that she would be too frightened to go on her own; when that fails to worry her, Angie suggests that she has the ability to move objects

> **CONTEXT**
>
> The Saatchi & Saatchi poster campaign for the Conservative Party in the run-up to the 1979 general election showed a queue of people under the heading 'Labour Isn't Working' (1978) and 'Labour Still Isn't Working' (1979) and is widely credited with helping the Conservatives to win the election and make Margaret Thatcher Prime Minister.

 CHECK THE NET

The Victoria and Albert Museum has a copy of the 'Labour Still Isn't Working Poster' and a short contextual essay about it. Go to **www.vam.ac.uk** and search for 'Labour Still Isn't Working' or search for museum reference number E.141-1986.

by thought alone and to see and hear a dead kitten. Kit is sceptical about this and her refusal to be intimidated leads to a fight which culminates in Kit showing Angie her menstrual blood and Angie licking it from Kit's finger. Joyce comes out and calls Angie in again; when there is no answer, Joyce swears at them and then goes back into the house.

The girls sit in silence for a while before Kit brings up the subject of the safest place to go in the event of a nuclear war. Angie hints that she is leaving anyway and, after another argument, eventually tells Kit that she is running away to her aunt in London. The girls reach an uneasy truce just as Joyce comes up to them and asks them in. She agrees that they can go to the cinema if Angie tidies her room. Angie is angry and goes off to do it very reluctantly. Joyce talks to Kit – it transpires that Kit wants to be a nuclear physicist and knows that she is clever – this makes Joyce prickly and defensive about Angie who comes back wearing a dress that is too small for her. This makes Joyce inexplicably angry, and Angie responds by picking up a brick to kill her mother (something she has talked about throughout the scene), Joyce fails to react and she and Kit run into the house to avoid the rain. Kit comes back out to fetch Angie in, and, on being told that Angie had put on the dress to kill her mother, remarks, 'Well you didn't, so' (Act 2, p. 45).

 CHECK THE BOOK

Charlotte Keatley's play *My Mother Said I Never Should* (1987) shares several formal properties with *Top Girls*, notably the use of adult actors to portray children, the rejection of a chronological structure and the opening scene featuring women of different historical periods.

COMMENTARY

When studying this scene it is important to remember that the two girls are being played by adults which presents a surreal stage picture of two grown women dressed as children hunched in a shelter. This will affect the audience's response to everything else that happens in the scene. It is clear from the beginning that Angie is slightly disturbed, and this will be stressed by the fact that the actress portraying her is an adult. Her responses to everything are heightened and she is very quick to anger and employ physical and verbal violence. She is also intrigued by sex and violence – which makes Kit's suggested film, *The Exterminator*, an inadvisable choice (and possibly a tongue-in-cheek one on Churchill's behalf). When the trip to the cinema is mooted Angie moves from a resigned sulkiness, 'She won't let me, will she?' (Act 2, p. 34), to taking out her frustration on Kit, first suggesting that Kit looks too young to get into an X-rated film, then that she would be too scared to go on her own. It is clear that even though Kit is much younger than Angie she is more mature, self-possessed and perceptive and that she will eventually grow apart from Angie. When Angie rather peevishly says that Joyce dislikes Kit, Kit calmly replies, 'It's you she doesn't like' (Act 2, p. 34), and the truth of this statement is verified by Joyce's behaviour during the remainder of the scene.

Kit's refusal to be scared by Angie's stories of dead cats and poltergeists leads to an extraordinary confrontation. Angie asserts that Kit is frightened of blood, and Kit reaches under her skirt and covers her finger in menstrual blood which she then brandishes at Angie: a literal and **metaphorical** assertion that she is a woman rather than the 'baby' that Angie likes to pretend she is. Angie then licks the blood from Kit's finger in a gesture which is both childish and sexual. When she tells Kit, 'You'll have to do that when I get mine' (Act 2, p. 36), she is simultaneously trying to reassert her authority and bind Kit closer to her – and once again, her efforts fail, as does her attempt to pretend that she has had sexual intercourse. At this point Joyce calls them in again, offering tea and chocolate biscuits: an expected interaction between an adult and children juxtaposed with the unexpectedness of Joyce swearing at Angie – using the same obscenity that Angie has just hurled at Kit – when they ignore her. This is a shocking moment in the play – a taboo word used not just in an attempt to shock (as in the case of Angie and Kit), but in anger and with real feeling. It is made more shocking by the fact that up to this point Joyce has been behaving in a typically maternal fashion. It is clear that Angie and Joyce are both very quick to anger and that this is probably one of the sources of tension between them.

Kit's talk of 'a war' (Act 2, p. 38) reflects the concern in the 1980s with nuclear weapons and the possibility of nuclear warfare. In the context of the play it also serves to underline the extent to which Kit is engaged with the wider world (unlike Angie, who is entirely focused on the familiar); it also adds background to her ambition to become a nuclear physicist confided to Joyce at the end of the scene. Joyce who, by her own admission, did not work hard at school and now regrets it, worries that Angie has no future unless someone

---

CONTEXT

Nuclear war between the USA and Britain and the Soviet Union was a real possibility in the 1970s and early 1980s. Both sides had armed themselves with nuclear weapons (many of the USA's were based in Britain) during the Cold War, a battle of two ideologies: capitalism (established in the USA and western Europe) and communism (established in the Soviet Union and eastern Europe).

CONTEXT

The James Bond
films and books
were a product of
the Cold War, as
were John Le
Carré's Smiley
series and the
song 'Two Tribes'
by Frankie Goes to
Hollywood.

marries her – another reminder that many women still depended on men for a degree of economic stability. Kit's and Angie's relevance to the rest of the play becomes apparent only towards the end of this scene when Angie mentions her plan to go to London to see her aunt, who 'gets people jobs' – the first hint of a link to Marlene and the Top Girls Employment Agency. Angie's obsession with her aunt, who she thinks is special, means that when she tells Kit that: 'I think I'm my aunt's child. I think my mother's really my aunt' (Act 2, p. 41) it seems an entirely characteristic piece of wishful thinking on Angie's part.

GLOSSARY

33	**an X** a film that is rated for adults only and thus one Kit and Angie are unlikely to be admitted to
	Ipswich large town in Suffolk, presumably the nearest place with a cinema
	Odeon a cinema within the Odeon cinema chain, used here as a generic term for cinema
38	**a war** judging from Kit's description of 'walking around with your skin dragging on the ground', they are wondering about the best place to go in the event of a nuclear war

ACT 2, SCENE 3, PAGES 45–53

- Win and Nell arrive for work at the Top Girls Employment Agency and discuss their weekend over coffee.
- They discuss their clients for the day; among them is a young woman who shows great promise.
- Marlene arrives and they congratulate her on her promotion. They all discuss Howard Kidd's reaction to the news. (He was Marlene's rival for the job.)
- Win interviews Louise, a woman in her forties who has put her job before her personal life, but never received recognition for it.

This scene introduces the audience to Marlene's colleagues, Win and Nell. They share her rejection of the traditional feminine aspirations of a husband and a family, preferring instead to focus on their careers. They disparage Howard Kidd – Marlene's rival for promotion – and discuss their career progressions: Nell is thinking of moving on, Win is happy for the moment. They are reviewing the day's clients when Marlene comes in and they offer their congratulations. Marlene asks Nell how she feels about having her as a boss and we discover that Nell also applied for the job. It is clear that Marlene takes her responsibilities seriously: she is interviewing a sick colleague's clients so that there is no backlog, and she checks on Win's and Nell's progress with their own clients. Win interviews Louise, an older woman who wants to move to a different company and enjoy the opportunities she has seen younger women have. Win's manner is similar to Marlene's: she is polite, businesslike and unafraid to ask difficult questions.

COMMENTARY

This scene further contextualises the exploration of women's experiences in the world of work. We see a parade of working women, starting with Win and Nell, Marlene's Top Girls colleagues, and Louise – who has been less fortunate than her younger peers. As in the first act, the women cover a broad spectrum and much would be lost in performance if the differences between the women were not observed and enacted. Although Win and Nell are evidently 'top girls', they are very different, and the women they go on to interview during this act reflect their differences. Win is having an affair with a married man, has spent the weekend at his home in the country and enjoyed herself enormously: 'It was like living together' (Act 2, p. 45).

Nell disapproves – not on moral grounds, but because she thinks Win is being taken advantage of – and her account of her own weekend reveals a much more self-sufficient person. Despite spending Friday night with one lover and Saturday with another, it was spending Sunday evening curled up with a mug of cocoa that she enjoyed the most. Yet, in spite of this, Nell still likes to boast that she could 'play house ace' if she chose to, but when Win suggests that Nell could get married and go on working, Nell

CHECK THE BOOK

David Mamet's 1983 play *Glengarry Glen Ross* is about a group of real-estate salesmen. Its all-male cast and their aggressive attitude towards their careers can be usefully compared to the all-female cast of *Top Girls* and the attitudes of the women in the Top Girls Employment Agency.

CHECK THE FILM
Glengarry Glen Ross (1992) is an adaptation of David Mamet's 1983 play. The high-pressure nature of the job puts the men – played by Al Pacino, Jack Lemmon and Alec Badwin – under constant stress and makes them competitive and insecure with each other. Their motto is 'ABC – Always Be Closing [the deal]' – an echo of Shona's indignant: 'I close don't I?' (Act 2, p. 61).

replies, 'or I could go on working and not marry him' (Act 2, p. 48). When the play was first performed this attitude was far more commonly associated with men and would have confirmed for some members of the audience that Nell was 'unnatural' (an accusation levelled at Marlene later in Act 2, and also frequently levelled at Margaret Thatcher during her time as Prime Minister). For other members of the original audience, it would confirm the idea that certain schools of feminism had led to women aping men's behaviour, rather than developing their own role models. Nell's ambition is demonstrated by the fact that she too had applied for the managing director's position, and by her frank admission to Marlene that 'I don't like coming second' (Act 2, p. 50). It is left to Win (who is generally a much softer character) to break the silence after this confession and to affirm that both women are pleased for Marlene and even more pleased that Howard was unsuccessful. Win's gentleness does not make her any less effective in her job – at least as far as the scene in which she interviews Louise suggests. Like Marlene, she asks direct, probing questions and is not afraid to give advice about Louise's presentation: 'You shouldn't talk too much at an interview' (Act 2, p. 53).

The extent to which Nell, Win and Marlene subvert gender norms is apparent in the way they discuss their male clients, using epithets like 'pretty', a word more commonly applied to women, to describe their male clients (Act 2, p. 50). The conjunction of 'pretty' (denoting attractive) with an unflattering expletive (presumably denoting ruthlessness) emphasises Nell's confidence in her role, and also in her relationship with Marlene: her language suggests that they are all modern women who evaluate men in the same terms as men use to judge each other. The ease with which she swears in front of Marlene (not appropriate in most boss–employee relationships) could indicate that she is challenging Marlene's authority by deliberately trying to provoke a confrontation, or perhaps that Marlene has already made it clear to them that she will continue to treat them as equals even though she is now their boss.

GLOSSARY

45–6	Mermaid, Iceberg, Marilyn, Esther's Baby different varieties of rose
46	Elvis Elvis Presley, iconic rock 'n' roll singer of the 1950s
	John Conteh former world light-heavyweight boxing champion, one of Britain's most popular sportsmen at the time
	bleeping a colloquial term, derived from the noise made by intercoms (inter-office communication system). The fact that Howard constantly bleeps the others for help suggests that he considers them to be his minions, and also that he cannot deal with situations on his own
47	Dymchurch small town on the south-east coast of England
48	Holden, Barker, Gardiner, Duke more varieties of rose
49	tube London Underground train service. Marlene is blaming a glitch in the service for her lateness
	Sussex county in the south of England

QUESTION

How does Churchill's use of colloquialisms enhance the authenticity of the **dialogue**?

ACT 2, SCENE 3, PAGES 53–66

- Angie arrives unannounced to visit Marlene.
- Mrs Kidd arrives to ask Marlene to give up the manager's position in favour of her husband.
- Nell interviews Shona – the promising candidate – and realises that her CV and answers are a tissue of lies.
- Win talks to Angie and tells her how she came to be working at Top Girls.
- Nell announces that Howard has had a heart attack.

When Angie first arrives Marlene mistakes her for a client, and even when she realises who she is, continues to bombard her with questions to establish why she's there. Mrs Kidd (Howard's wife) bursts in during their talk (Marlene fails to recognise her) and asks Marlene if she will resign her post in favour of Howard. Marlene refuses; Mrs Kidd abuses her and storms off. Marlene's behaviour only confirms Angie's opinion of her greatness and she promises to wait in the office until Marlene finishes work.

The scene changes to Nell interviewing the ambitious Shona (the same client she spoke to Win about earlier and whom she hopes to persuade to join the company). Initially, Shona seems too good to be true: she works in a male-dominated field and is very successful but, when Nell asks her for more detail about a typical day, her answer makes it clear that she has been lying. However, even after she has been exposed she is adamant that she could do such a job which suggests that she has the ambition necessary to succeed.

Win talks to Angie while she eats her lunch and tells her how she came to be working at the Agency (and about her nervous breakdown). Angie falls asleep and Win ends up talking to herself, which is how Nell finds her when she comes in to break the news of Howard's heart attack. Marlene comes to check on Angie and they discuss her prospects: Marlene's predictions for her are as pessimistic as Joyce's.

CHECK THE BOOK

Michael Frayn's 2002 novel, *Spies*, focuses around two families in wartime suburbia. Stephen, a boy at the time, struggles to understand the adult world and its secrets.

Commentary

Angie's arrival changes the tone of the scene: it introduces the personal into the workplace (a theme continued by Mrs Kidd's appearance and Win's story). She arrives at the Top Girls office and announces to Marlene, 'It's me. I've come' (Act 2, p. 53), as if Marlene were expecting her. This is so far from the truth that Marlene initially mistakes her for a client, but does not falter when she realises who it is. There are no stage directions to dictate how the rest of the encounter with Angie should be played – Marlene might be genuinely pleased to see her, and curious about what she plans to do; or she might cover her surprise and awkwardness by being especially enthusiastic, particularly in the delivery of the line 'You came by yourself, that's fun' (Act 2, p. 54). It seems likely that the conversation will become awkward once she realises that Angie is not down for the day, and that 'I do think Joyce might have phoned me. It's like her' is an expression of both annoyance at what she sees as Joyce's thoughtlessness and a way of covering up her own embarrassment at not having seen Angie for so long (Act 2, p. 55). The short exchanges (usually not more than a sentence each) emphasise Angie's strangeness and Marlene's lack of familiarity with the teenager.

The sudden entrance of Mrs Kidd (Howard's wife) provides a distraction and, once again, Marlene is initially very polite, although she makes it clear that she has only five minutes to spare. Again, we see Marlene's professional side as she listens to Mrs Kidd's complaints and tries to placate her: 'Business life is full of little setbacks', 'I'll consult him over any decisions affecting his department' (Act 2, p. 58). Mrs Kidd's represents the traditional **patriarchal** point of view that men are superior to women, and that women should sacrifice everything for their well-being. Twice she refers to the natural/normal order of things: first when she remarks, 'I think if it was a man [who had been promoted over him] he'd get over it as something normal' (Act 2, p. 58) and again at the end of her interview with Marlene, 'It's not that easy, a man of Howard's age. You don't care. I thought he was going too far but he's right ... You'll end up miserable and lonely' (Act 2, p. 59). Eventually Mrs Kidd's veiled and not so veiled insults about 'unnatural' women provoke Marlene to ask her to leave in no uncertain terms (Act 2, p. 59).

Nell's interview with Shona complements the earlier scene in which Win interviews Louise. Shona is young, while Louise is middle aged; Shona has no experience, while Louise has a great deal of it; but Shona is so ambitious that she will lie in order to get a job, whereas Louise is too principled to behave in such a ruthless way. Shona's interview marks the end of the act's exploration of the different stages of women's liberation in the workplace. Louise, the eldest woman, makes it clear that she has 'lived for that company, I've given my life really you could say' without ever getting the recognition she deserves and being promoted to senior management (Act 2, p. 51). She describes the new breed of woman, who she seems to fear and envy in equal measure, as 'attractive, well-dressed', whereas she says of herself, 'I pass as a man at work' (Act 2, p. 52). Marlene is clearly one of this new breed: she has achieved senior management status without passing as a man or, at least, not on the surface. As she tells her dinner guests, 'I don't wear trousers in the office. / I could but I don't' (Act 1, p. 8). Nell is

> **CONTEXT**
>
> The views expressed here chime with those of the critics who thought that *Top Girls* was an 'anti-feminist' feminist play, because it showed women in conflict rather than in harmony. The idea that there is a 'natural/normal' way for men and women to behave is a perennial one which feminists continually challenge.

CHECK THE FILM

Wall Street (1987), directed by Oliver Stone, starring Martin and Charlie Sheen and Michael Douglas, takes a critical look at America and the aggressive capitalist instincts of Gordon Gecko (a ruthless businessman played by Douglas) and his influence over stockbroker Bud Fox (Charlie Sheen).

another generation again, happy to use men for her own pleasure, but not commit, and Shona represents a new and unknown future where ambition might replace experience and talent completely. If Marlene, as Nell points out, has more ambition than Howard, it seems that Shona might have more ambition than both Marlene and Nell (Act 2, p. 46).

When Win confides her story to the sleeping Angie, it becomes clear why she sympathises with Louise and is kind to Angie: she understands what it is like to suffer. Her story provides us with another perspective on the price of being a 'top girl': alcoholism, mental health problems and a history of abusive relationships. However, she is not so sympathetic when Nell announces that Howard has had a heart attack: 'Too much butter, too much smoke' (Act 2, p. 66). The togetherness that Win, Louise and Angie display in the final minutes of this scene is dispelled when Marlene calls Angie 'a bit thick' and pronounces, 'She's not going to make it' – suggesting that solidarity exists only among other top girls (Act 2, p. 66), and that their success will always be at the expense of the less able, less ambitious and less ruthless.

GLOSSARY

55	**Madame Tussaud's** tourist attraction full of waxworks of celebrities
	day return return rail ticket valid only for one day
60	**Too many late nights, me** Nell's comment is meant to imply that Shona looks very young for her age. Presumably, despite being a similar age, Nell looks much older
	six basic and three commission Her basic salary is £6,000 and she earns an average of £3,000 on top of that on commission from her sales. Commission is usually a percentage of the overall sale price
	titular management status the title of manager without management responsibility
61	**closing situation** a colloquial way of referring to the completion of a business transaction. In Shona's case it is the process of converting a verbal agreement (to buy) into a written agreement
63	**M1** motorway in England running from London to the north

64	**sitting in my chair / eating my porridge** an allusion to the fairytale *Goldilocks and the Three Bears*. A joking reference to the fact that Angie is sitting at Win's desk
	knackered colloquial expression for being tired
65	**CSE** Certificate of Secondary Education. In the English education system CSEs were an alternative to Ordinary Level certificates (Os) and were considered to be less prestigious
	inside colloquial English expression for being in prison

ACT 3, PAGES 67–77

- The action takes place a year earlier than the preceding acts. Marlene is visiting Joyce and Angie on a Sunday evening and has brought them presents.
- It transpires that Angie invited Marlene and pretended that she was doing it on her mother's behalf. Both sisters are cross that they have been fooled and are awkward with each other.
- Kit comes round to play with Angie who refuses to go out because she is so captivated by Marlene.
- Joyce tells Marlene that she has separated from her husband, Frank.
- Angie is sent to bed and the sisters start to drink.

Marlene has come to visit Joyce and Angie and it is clear that this is a rare occurrence from her comments about how big Angie has grown since she last saw her. Among the presents Marlene has brought is the dress that Angie puts on in Act 2, Scene 2: this establishes that the act is a flashback to an earlier point. (The stage direction confirms this: '*A year earlier*'.) Joyce's reception of her sister is surprisingly formal, presumably because she was not expecting her; Marlene is surprised by this as she thought she had been invited. It becomes clear that Angie invited Marlene but pretended she was doing so on Joyce's behalf. We gather from this that Angie's fascination with Marlene – so evident in Act 2, Scenes

 CHECK THE BOOK

The Homecoming by Harold Pinter was first performed at the Aldwych Theatre, London, in 1965. A satirical and disturbing look at the idealisation of the home and the woman's place within it, the play concerns the return of Teddy, an academic at an American university, to his childhood home in a working-class district of London. He and his wife are initially given a hostile reception by his family and the play ends with Teddy returning to America while his wife stays behind to work as a prostitute.

CHECK THE FILM

The Homecoming (1973), a film adaptation of the play, was directed by Peter Hall (director of the first stage production); it has several members of the original cast.

2 and 3 – is a longstanding one. This is confirmed by Angie's refusal to play with Kit – the allure of Marlene is too strong. Joyce tells Marlene all the news from the village – including the fact that she separated from her husband, Frank, three years ago. Marlene tells Angie about working in America. Joyce sends Angie to bed and Marlene promises to go up and say goodnight.

COMMENTARY

Although *Top Girls* is far from being conventional in structure, the final act draws together some of the apparently unrelated **narrative** arcs of the preceding acts, notably Joyce's conflicted feelings towards Angie, Angie's fixation with Marlene, and Marlene's ambition, spurred on by her desire to avoid following in the footsteps of her mother's and sister's 'wasted' lives. The scenario of a successful sibling revisiting their home town is a common theme in post-war British drama offering the opportunity for conflict, resolution and giving the protagonists a chance to develop a fresh understanding or come to accommodation with the family they left behind. Churchill, however, flouts the convention of providing a neat resolution: the sisters are, if anything, more divided by the end of the play than they were at the beginning. This act also offers a glimpse of what life is like for those who do not move to London and become Top Girls. (Joyce does not even have a telephone in the house.)

CHECK THE FILM
Brassed Off (1996), directed by Mark Herman, depicts a young woman returning to the mining village she grew up in to assess whether or not to close the mine. The film demonstrates the close-knit nature of miners and mining (signified by the colliery brass band).

Joyce's ungracious behaviour at the beginning of this act would seem to confirm the impression given in Act 2, Scene 2 that she veers between brisk affection and truculence. She accepts Marlene's gifts grudgingly, partly because of her embarrassment at being caught unawares 'with the place in a mess' but also because she resents her sister's extravagance (showering them both with expensive presents) (Act 3, p. 68). She is torn between indulging Angie's pleasure at receiving the gifts and seeing her glamorous aunt and experiencing understandable resentment at Marlene's wealth and popularity with Angie (easy enough to explain given the infrequency of her visits and lavishness of her offerings). At this point in the play, an audience might assume that Marlene's infrequent visits are as much a result of Joyce's unfriendly behaviour, as they are a product of Marlene's hectic lifestyle.

However, as the act unfolds, Joyce's stiffness becomes more understandable. The short exchanges between the sisters in this section make use of **sub-text** and draw on the audience's understanding of the working-class/middle-class divide. Both sisters grew up as part of a working-class family in a working-class community. Joyce is still a part of that community, not just because she has remained in the same place, but because she earns her living doing menial work. Marlene's wealth and tastes – displayed at the dinner party and in the gifts she brings Angie and Joyce – show that she has joined the ranks of the middle classes.

Joyce's defensive comment, 'We had our dinner dinnertime', has a multitude of implications for a British audience. On the surface it is an apparently neutral comment warning Marlene not to expect an evening meal – either because they have already eaten it or, and more likely, that they had their hot meal at lunchtime as is traditional in Britain on a Sunday (Act 3, p. 68). Joyce's choice of words is also significant: traditionally in England, the working class ate their main meal, dinner, at midday in order to fortify themselves for the rest of their working day (which usually consisted of manual labour) and referred to the break as 'dinner-time'. In middle- and upper-class households, the main meal was eaten in the evening and was also referred to as a dinner. It is possible, therefore, that Joyce is stressing to Marlene that she continues to uphold the traditions in which they were both brought up, and that the remark is therefore a pointed one about Marlene's transcendence of her origins.

Joyce's assumption that Marlene does not take sugar is another example of this, 'taking care of yourself' being a luxury that only the wealthier classes can afford (Act 3, p. 68). It is important to remember that these are all assumptions, and ones which Marlene has done nothing to foster by her words or actions in the scene – it also allows the actor playing Marlene to get a laugh from the audience when she asks Joyce for the sugar (Act 3, p. 70). Joyce's anger and discomfort at not being able to appear hospitable has the unfortunate effect of making her behave more inhospitably. The inordinate length of time they spend talking about food – 'You could have an egg', 'I'd have got a cake if she'd told me' – assumes

CHECK THE BOOK

David Storey's *In Celebration*, first performed at the Royal Court Theatre in 1969, explores the conflicts in the Shaw family, when the three sons return for their parents' fortieth wedding anniversary. Their father was a miner who was determined that they should be educated in order to achieve a better life than his own, but his sacrifice is largely unappreciated.

almost farcical proportions, but speaks volumes about British reserve and the skirmishes conducted under the guise of politeness (Act 3, pp. 68–9), even among family.

This act shows Marlene at a disadvantage for the first time in the play. There does not seem to be much love lost between the sisters, and all Marlene's attempts to make pleasant conversation are rebuffed. For example, when she tells Joyce how much she likes being out of London and being in the fresh air, Joyce asks, 'What sort of air you get in London then?' (Act 3, p. 70). In another exchange, Marlene, who is doing her best to be conciliatory, attempts a show of modesty, saying, 'I'm not clever, just pushy', to which Joyce replies 'True enough' (Act 3, p. 72). There is much comic mileage to be had in this scene and the actors might choose to really exploit it in an exchange like this. As the action progresses it becomes apparent that Joyce's sharpness is partly a defence mechanism against all the hardships in her life (looking after a difficult child, separating from her husband, having several different jobs to earn enough for them to live on) and partly due to her fears for Angie's future, which is a recurrent motif in the play: 'She hasn't an idea in her head what she wants to do. / Lucky to get anything' (Act 3, p. 72).

Despite Joyce's harsh words, Angie displays more animation and intelligence in this scene than at any other point during the play. She clearly adores Marlene, not just because of the presents she has brought on this occasion, but because she associates her with a life of glamour and extravagance, as evidenced by her memory of her ninth birthday in which Marlene and the pink cake are linked by their deliciousness and novelty (Act 3, p. 74). The fact that she has memorised and kept Marlene's postcard from America, her awareness of the relatively new phenomenon of frequent transatlantic travel, and even her copying of stories about politicians from newspapers, suggest that she is more engaged with everyday life than Joyce thinks. It also gives her something in common with Shona: both have been seduced by the glamour of the 'high-flier' lifestyle peddled by the media.

GLOSSARY

75   **Concorde** an aircraft that travelled faster than the speed of sound and therefore reduced the journey time of transatlantic travel; decommissioned in 2003 amid safety fears

      Laker British airline, no longer operating

76   **lapwings** a species of wading bird, also known as a plover

CONTEXT

Deborah Findlay, who played Joyce in the original production and in the 1991 revival, used issues of *Cosmopolitan* from 1980 and 1981 to help remind the cast of the messages being sent to women through these magazines at the time: 'it was extraordinary to look and see how many of the articles were to do with "high fliers" and "women making it on their own"'.

ACT 3, PAGES 77–87

- Joyce and Marlene discuss Angie and drink whisky.
- Marlene reveals that she has been to visit their ageing mother.
- We discover Angie is Marlene's daughter. The sisters quarrel and make up.
- They discuss the new Thatcher administration and argue about politics.
- Joyce goes to bed leaving Marlene to sleep on the sofa, where she is disturbed by a frightened Angie.

Marlene goes up to wish Angie goodnight; when she comes back Joyce asks about Angie's secret and Marlene refuses to tell her. This leads to a discussion of Angie generally and Joyce reveals that she has been in a special needs class for the last two years. Joyce is annoyed when she finds out that Marlene has been to visit their mother; and even more annoyed when Marlene expresses sympathy for the difficult life she had. Joyce's life is also a struggle, and she is angry with Marlene for leaving and jealous of her glamorous lifestyle. It emerges that Angie is actually Marlene's daughter, and that when Marlene announced that she would give her up, Joyce adopted her. The full extent of the sisters' rancour begins to emerge at this point. Marlene threatens to take Angie away; Joyce condemns her for abandoning Angie in the first place, although Marlene replies, 'You were quick enough to take her. ... You couldn't have one so you took mine' (Act 3, p. 79). Joyce denies this and reveals that Angie was a difficult baby who cried all the time and that when Joyce did become pregnant, she was so exhausted she had a miscarriage.

They move into a discussion about the new political and economic climate: Joyce is a socialist and thinks it is wrong for people to have more money than they need. Marlene is a capitalist and believes that everyone can make money if they put their minds to it and work hard. Joyce asks what happens to people like Angie in a society like that and Marlene cannot answer satisfactorily. They go to bed, just as Marlene is going to sleep, Angie comes down having had a bad dream, she calls Marlene 'Mum' twice (it is not clear whether this is because she mistakes her for Joyce or because what she has overheard has confirmed her wish) and the second time Marlene corrects her: once again denying her maternal status. Angie's response is to repeat one word, 'Frightening' (Act 3, p. 87).

COMMENTARY

The revelation that Angie is Marlene's daughter puts a whole new light on Marlene's behaviour during the first and second acts. Like Nijo, Griselda and Joan, she has known what it feels like to give up a child. Joyce's attitude towards Marlene and Angie is now much more understandable as the sacrifices she made for them both are revealed in this scene. It seems that Marlene assuaged her guilt about leaving them by convincing herself that it was what Joyce wanted, 'turned out lucky for you, didn't it? (Act 3, p. 79). Joyce's retort, 'Turned out all right for you by the look of you. You'd be getting a few less thousand a year', points up the similarities between their situation and that of Isabella Bird and her sister, Hennie. (Hennie's willingness to stay at home and play the dutiful daughter gave Isabella the freedom she needed.) Marlene points out that Joyce was happy enough to take Angie at the time, and she has always refused to accept any financial support from her which would have made her life easier. Marlene's offer to take Angie away with her comes as something of a surprise given the infrequency of her visits (and her unenthusiastic reception of Angie in Act 2, Scene 3). Joyce refuses, asserting her claim to Angie in spite of their difficult relationship, 'She's my child' (Act 3, p. 80).

Joyce's revelation that she had a miscarriage because Angie was such a demanding baby momentarily wrong-foots Marlene, who protests that she never knew about it; she retaliates by revealing that she has had two abortions and 'it wasn't a problem' (Act 3, p. 81). The fact Marlene then bursts into tears, suggests that perhaps this assertion is not entirely true, and that she feels guiltier about leaving Joyce and Angie then she likes to pretend. She rejects Joyce's attempt to comfort her, 'let me cry, I like it' (Act 3, p. 81), admitting a degree of vulnerability at odds with her professional demeanour in Act 2, and the social side she displayed in Act 1. This emotional confrontation over, the sisters, mellowed by whisky, discuss common ground: their relationships with men. Joyce threw out her husband because he had affairs and tried to stop her going out – even to attend evening classes: she would now 'sooner do without' (Act 3, p. 83). Marlene still wants to find a man who does not expect the 'high-flying lady' to turn into the 'little woman' (Act 3, p. 83).

Just as it looks as if they will settle down for an amicable evening, the conversation turns to politics. Unsurprisingly, Marlene is a great fan of Margaret Thatcher – 'She's a tough lady' – and of the way in which she is trying to dismantle the welfare state to make people independent and ambitious (Act 3, p. 84), regardless of the privations this causes. Joyce, a staunch socialist, questions the idea that Thatcher's promotion is a sign of progress for women: 'What good's first woman if it's her?' (Act 3, p. 84). She also challenges the idea that the 1980s will be 'stupendous' for everyone: 'you've got on, nothing's changed for most people / has it? (Act 3, pp. 83, 85). The argument grows in intensity and becomes personal, Marlene claiming that 'I hate the working class' of which Joyce is clearly a member, and Joyce declaring that when the socialists overthrow capitalism, 'don't be round here when it happens because if someone's kicking you I'll just laugh' (Act 3, pp. 85, 86). For all her ruthless, capitalist instincts, Marlene turns out to be the more conciliatory of the two, twice trying to end the argument without attributing blame: 'I don't mean anything personal. I don't believe in class', and, at the end of the night, telling Joyce, 'I didn't really mean all that' (Act 3, pp. 86, 87). Joyce rejects these attempts, first asking how the new system will care for people like Angie who are

QUESTION

How sincere do you think is Marlene's offer to take Angie away?

CHECK THE BOOK

Willy Russell's *Educating Rita*, first performed at the (Donmar) Warehouse in 1980, explores a working-class woman's attempts at self-improvement by enrolling for an Open University degree. Her desire to change results in her separating from her husband in the same way that Joyce has. There is a film adaptation of the play, starring Julie Walters.

CHECK THE BOOK
Andrea Dunbar's
The Arbor, first
performed at the
Royal Court Theatre
in 1980 (written
when the
playwright was 18),
is a semi-
autobiographical
tale of a girl who
lives on a large
council estate
outside Bradford,
gets pregnant at 15,
struggles to break
free of an abusive
relationship and
make a life for her
and her child. In the
context of *Top Girls*,
The Arbor offers a
view of life in a
decaying industrial
area, and a glimpse
of how Marlene's
life might have
been had she kept
Angie and stayed in
her hometown.

'stupid, lazy and frightened'; and finally refusing Marlene's apology and plea for friendship (Act 3, p. 87).

Joyce's rejection of Marlene is followed by Marlene's rejection of Angie, both in this scene, and in the future. Although she tells Joyce that Angie will 'be all right' (Act 3, p. 86) in the new Thatcherite world, her words ring hollow in the light of what we know happens to her a year later when she turns up at Marlene's office and Marlene tells her colleagues, 'She's not going to make it' (Act 2, p. 66). By that time she has left school with no job to go to, no idea of what she would like to do and no qualifications (Act 2, p. 65). This outcome is clearly signposted when Angie comes back downstairs having had a nightmare:

ANGIE: Mum?
MARLENE: Angie? What's the matter?
ANGIE: Mum?
MARLENE: No, she's gone to bed. It's Aunty Marlene.
ANGIE: Frightening.

(Act 3, p. 87)

Marlene not only rejects her role as Angie's mother – understandable given the sacrifices Joyce has made to occupy this role – she offers Angie little comfort, reverting instead to her businesslike manner: 'Did you have a bad dream? ... Well, you're awake now, aren't you pet?' The play ends on the word 'Frightening' (Act 3, p. 87), offering a bleak vision of the future of Angie, Joyce and all the people who lack the ambition and the determination to succeed in the new meritocracy. Max Stafford-Clark (the director of the first production) sums up the feeling he wanted to provoke in the audience:

> The moment when Angie says 'Frightening' is incredibly frightening on stage. The play is also frightening, to use Angie's word, and frighteningly prophetic, written on the threshold of Thatcher's eighties, as it posits the perspective that those who are less talented, those who are weaker, will go the wall.
>
> (Goodman in Rabillard (1998), p. 96)

GLOSSARY

77	**remedial class** term current at the time to describe classes specifically tailored for children with learning difficulties
80	**sunshine** affectionate term, used sarcastically in this instance
81	**grizzle** colloquial term meaning cry
84	**Maggie** Margaret Thatcher
	monetarism economic policy which holds that the money supply in an economy is the main factor in controlling inflation, and therefore that controlling the money supply can determine the growth of a country's economy
86	**blanquette de veau** veal covered in a cream sauce, a French dish
	Siberia area of northern Russia. Under the Soviet regime, intellectuals, dissidents and other 'aliens' were sent to labour camps, some of which were in Siberia
	flying picket person who moved from one picket line to another. Ordinarily a picket line (a line of workers blocking the entrance to a place of work during a strike) would consist of striking workers from the workplace in question; during the 1984 miners' strike, pickets would drive all over the country in order to defend picket lines from the police
	Reagan Ronald Reagan, President of the USA 1980–8, started out as a minor actor in Hollywood, predominantly in westerns. His time in power was distinguished by an extremely conservative attitude towards law and order, drugs and 'public morality'
	reds communists

CHECK THE FILM

In *Secrets and Lies* (1996), directed by Mike Leigh, Hortense (Marianne Jean Baptiste) is a successful black woman who finds out she is adopted and traces her birth mother only to find she is a white working-class woman called Rose (Brenda Blethyn). Although she is pleased to meet Hortense, Rose does not want to admit that she is her daughter to her friends and family. The truth comes out as does the fact that Rose's brother Maurice and his wife have been unable to have children.

CHECK THE BOOK

Ronald Reagan's values are criticised in detail in Tony Kushner's play *Angels in America* (1990–2).

EXTENDED COMMENTARIES

TEXT 1 – ACT 1, PAGES 2–6

From 'It was always the men who used to get so drunk' to 'Anyway, I'm a heresy myself'.

This scene takes place near the beginning of the dinner party, just after Pope Joan's arrival. The women begin to discuss their different experiences, and in doing so reveal the differences in their religious

CONTEXT

An agnostic is someone who is undecided about whether or not God exists, as opposed to an atheist who denies the existence of God or any divine influence.

CONTEXT

From the sixteenth century onwards Britain (and other nations) claimed for itself so-called 'undiscovered' lands, exploiting their natural resources and subjecting the indigenous people to slavery, conversion to Christianity (in the case of Europeans, Islam in the case of the Ottoman Empire), the confiscation of property and physical abuse.

beliefs and cultural practices. In addition to Joan (a Catholic), the other guests present are Nijo (a Buddhist), Isabella (Church of England) and Marlene (an agnostic). Nijo's retelling of her induction into the Emperor's service, and the sake ritual involved, prompts Isabella to observe that sake is '[q]uite fortifying after a day in the wet' (Act 1, p. 2). In doing so she seems to miss the point that it is the ritual that is important and, in this case, the break with the ritual, rather than the properties of the drink itself. This is characteristic of Isabella's stance throughout the dinner: a citizen of Britain at the height of its imperial/colonial powers, she has a slightly condescending attitude to other cultures, religions and historical periods. Despite her desire to travel and experience other ways of living, she automatically assumes that the British way is the most sensible and rational, even if it is not for her. For example, when Nijo is describing her life as a Buddhist nun, Isabella remarks: 'I tried to understand Buddhism when I was in Japan but all this birth and death succeeding each other through eternities just filled me with the most profound melancholy. I do like something more active' (Act 1, p. 6).

By 'active', Isabella means a religion in which people must react to events and strive for goodness and salvation (by good works, for example), rather than practising the passive acceptance of one's fate as Nijo does. Churchill does not encourage us to judge Isabella too harshly for her behaviour however: as a child of the Victorian age she will have had the greatness of the British Empire inculcated into her all her life and thus has the brisk manner and stoicism typical of British men and women of the age. Instead her behaviour reminds us that even a progressive woman like her cannot escape some of the prejudices of her era.

In the same way, Nijo is confused by the western women's lack of interest in ceremony and ritual, and by their inability to understand her acceptance of her role, first as a child concubine, then as a wandering nun. She cannot understand why Marlene gets angry about their mistreatment, or the mistreatment of others, because Buddhism preaches tolerance and acceptance of events (Act 1, p. 5). Her description of Japanese court culture emphasises the highly formal, ceremonial nature of her life there. Similarly, her language is characterised by politeness and **euphemism**, rather than by the very blunt speech used by Marlene. This is most apparent when Nijo is describing her invitation to become one of the Emperor's concubines. He 'said, "Let the wild goose come to me this spring."':

NIJO: Well I was only fourteen and I knew he meant something but I didn't know what. He sent me an eight-layered gown and I sent it back. So when the time came I did nothing but cry. My thin gowns were badly ripped. But even that morning when he left / – he'd a green robe with a scarlet lining and

MARLENE: Are you saying he raped you?

NIJO: very heavily embroidered trousers, I already felt different about him. It made me uneasy. No, of course not, Marlene, I belonged to him, it was what I was brought up for from a baby. I soon found I was sad he stayed away.

     (Act 1, pp. 2–3)

CHECK THE BOOK

Cloud Nine (1985), also written by Caryl Churchill and directed by Max Stafford-Clark, juxtaposes two different historical epochs – Victorian Africa and contemporary 1970s London – to reveal the history of gender and racial oppression. However, as with *Top Girls*, Churchill suggests that things are more complicated than they appear.

Nijo enjoyed being wooed by subtle poetry, and being able to trace her rise in social status through the thinness of the silk she was allowed to wear (hence her constant references to the number of layers in her garments and those of the Emperor). She prides herself on being cultured and high-born and because of this we are able to appreciate what a sacrifice it must have been for her to give up all this for the life of an itinerant nun. Unlike Isabella and Joan, she was quite content with her life as laid out for her by her father and the Emperor, and it was only rejection that forced her to seek another path: 'I can't say I enjoyed my rough life. What I enjoyed most was being the Emperor's favourite / and wearing thin silk' (Act 1, p. 4).

There is a great deal of overlapping dialogue during this section of the play, principally because Isabella, Marlene and Nijo are the most **loquacious** of the dinner guests and have the most in common, having travelled and experienced different cultures. Their constant flow of talk and banter is in complete contrast to Gret, who, during this scene, replies to any attempts to draw her into the conversation

CHECK THE BOOK

Taking Stock (2007), by Max Stafford-Clark and Philip Roberts, discusses the development of *Cloud Nine*, and another Churchill play, *Serious Money*, in particular the research done by the company on attitudes towards women in the Victorian and contemporary periods.

with a one-word answer. This is not to say that Gret is a minor figure in this scene, simply that she makes her cultural background and feelings clear by non-linguistic means (see **Critical approaches: Characterisation** for more on Gret and her behaviour).

TEXT 2 – ACT 2, SCENE 3, PAGES 50–3

From 'Now Louise, hello' to 'Good for you.'

This short interview scene between Win, one of Marlene's colleagues, and Louise, a 46-year-old middle manager, offers the audience an insight into the women at work outside the Top Girls Agency. It also provides a means of comparing Win's interviewing technique with Marlene's: if Marlene's is appreciably better it goes some way to explaining why she is top of the Top Girls. In terms of dramatic practice it is also an excellent example of meaning being exchanged on a **sub-textual** level, or below the surface of what is actually being said. The pacing of this scene is interesting. At first glance, we might expect the short exchanges that make up the first two pages to proceed at a rapid pace, and then for Louise's longer answers, when she begins to unburden herself, to slow down the scene. A director might well choose to play it this way, but it is equally possible that, given Louise's reluctance to open up, the dialogue might move quite slowly at first, and then speed up as Louise starts to reveal more.

Win's opening gambit, 'Now Louise, hello, I have your details here' (Act 2, p. 50), is friendly – certainly more friendly than Marlene's opening in her interview with Jeanine, 'Right Jeanine, you are Jeanine aren't you?' (Act 2, p. 30) – and professional. This might reflect her personal style – she seems to be the kindest of the three colleagues – but will also reflect the fact that she is speaking to an older woman with a relatively high-status job, while Marlene was speaking to a younger woman in a low-status one. The fact that Win is more polite in her approach does not mean she is any less probing in her questions, if anything she asks more personal questions than Marlene does, but she builds up to them gradually. 'You've been very loyal to the one job' is a clear invitation for Louise to explain why, after so many years, she wants to find another job; and when Louise declines this opportunity, simply confirming Win's statement, 'Yes I have', Win is obliged to rephrase the question in order to find out more (Act 2, p. 50).

In the text, this is the first indication of the extent of Louise's formality and stiffness, qualities that in production might be suggested by her clothes, mannerisms and body language. In the 2002 production of the play, the actor playing Louise was dressed in dowdy clothes that made her look much older than 46; she sat very upright, keeping her handbag on her knee and constantly pushing up her glasses. All this contributed to the impression of Louise as someone who is old-fashioned and stuffy, a complete contrast to the quick-witted, glamorously dressed women at the Agency. Louise's behaviour thus far indicates to Win that she will have to alter her technique if she is to find out what she needs to know: Win's questions become more direct and personal, asking exactly how old she is, and being brutally honest about it being 'a handicap' (Act 2, p. 51).

Louise's answer, 'Nothing like that', to Win's question about 'any reason why you're leaving that wouldn't appear on the form' demonstrates the sub-textual level at which the interview is working (Act 2, p. 51). Louise understands that she is being asked whether she has had an affair that has ended badly, or has perhaps been taking bribes or stealing from the company. The suspicion of an affair is made more explicit in Win's second formulation of the question: 'No long term understandings come to a sudden end, making for an insupportable atmosphere?' Louise's reluctance to candidly acknowledge any of these possibilities is another sign of her repressed nature; she is able to hide behind Win's tactful formulations (Act 2, p. 51). When she finally begins to talk about her reasons for wanting to change, she becomes a much more sympathetic character. She has been a victim of her own perfectionism and modest nature: 'Nobody notices me, I don't expect it, I don't attract attention by making mistakes, everyone takes it for granted that my work will be perfect' (Act 2, p. 52).

Louise's sudden confession, her quietly expressed bitterness for the way she has been treated, and the way she has sacrificed her life for others can be paralleled with Mrs Kidd, who makes a fleeting

 CHECK THE BOOK

Interviews, or question-and-answer scenes, are often used in plays to provide lots of information very quickly. They can also tell us a lot about the social conventions at work in the world of the play. For example, in Pinter's *The Birthday Party* (1958), two men reduce a third to a nervous breakdown by asking him a series of questions he cannot possibly answer. This, and the tone they ask the questions in, communicates to an audience that something unusual is going on.

QUESTION

What is Churchill trying to tell us about feminism in this section?

appearance in the following scene. Both women pride themselves on their supporting roles, Louise in the workplace and Mrs Kidd in the home; both resent the way they have been taken advantage of – despite taking on the role voluntarily; and both seem to believe that men are superior to women and are complicit in their own oppression.

Like Marlene, Louise focuses on the individual, herself, rather than women collectively, and she has internalised male values to the extent that she boasts 'I think I pass as a man at work' (Act 2, p. 52). Given that she has failed to achieve the same status as the men she works with this seems unlikely: although she may *act* like a man, she has not benefited from it, merely alienated herself from other women. (Paradoxically, of course, outside work she has continued to behave exactly as unmarried women of a certain age were expected to in caring for her elderly mother.) When asked if she is the only woman at work, she replies, 'Apart from the girls, yes', thereby separating herself from the other women workers who are presumably in clerical positions rather than management ones (Act 2, p. 52). Unlike the women in the dinner-party scene, who celebrate each other's successes and commiserate with each other's setbacks, Louise has an ambivalent attitude towards the new breed of career woman (typified by Marlene and her Top Girls): '[T]here is a kind of woman who is thirty now who grew up in a different climate. They are not so careful. They take themselves for granted. I have had to justify existence every minute, and I have done so' (Act 2, p. 52).

There is a clear feeling of bitterness here, directed not at the **patriarchal** structures which have determined her life, but at the new women whose journey to the top has been easier, or who have made their lives easier by adopting typically male characteristics in order to succeed in business. The competitive spirit displayed by Marlene, Win and Nell is also present in Louise, but has warped into resentment rather than celebration. Mrs Kidd's warning to Marlene, 'You'll end up miserable and lonely', is already Louise's fate. There is the implication that the same ending might await the new generation of successful career women if they, like Marlene, choose their careers over family and long-term relationships

(Act 2, p. 59). This possibility is strengthened by the 'success story' Win later tells Angie (see Act 2, p. 65), and which is hinted at in this scene when she confesses to Louise that she drinks (Act 2, p. 53).

TEXT 3 – ACT 2, SCENE 3, PAGES 60–3

From 'Is this right? You are Shona?' to '... I bet you.'

This is the third interview scene in the play and suggests, through its similarities with Marlene's interview with Jeanine, that Nell may be Marlene's natural heir. We already know that she also applied for the managing director's post, and that she is highly ambitious and ruthless, and now we see her interviewing a young woman who turns out to be equally ruthless and ambitious. Shona has already been mentioned in the opening to this scene when Nell announces that she is seeing a lady who 'thinks she can sell' later that afternoon, and that she looks as if she will be a 'tough bird like us' (Act 2, p. 48). In fact she turns out to be a 19-year-old who has never had a job before, but who is defiant and unphased when her lack of experience is exposed.

The interview itself is difficult to interpret on the page because there are no stage directions to suggest what Shona looks like, how she behaves or at what point Nell realises that it is all 'a pack of lies' (Act 2, p. 63). The way in which Shona repeats everything Nell says suggests that she does not have the fluent patter we might expect from a salesperson, and also that she is strangely lacking in confidence for someone who spends a lot of time on the road. Perhaps Nell realises from the moment she sees Shona that she is not what she claims to be, but decides to see how far Shona's bravado will carry her. If Nell is really convinced by the 19-year-old – until she gives the fantasy description of her day – then Nell herself seems lacking in the perceptive qualities demonstrated by both Marlene and Win when interviewing the other clients.

QUESTION

Do you think Shona and Nell are similar as characters?

Unlike Marlene and Win, Nell begins her interview informally with a joke, apparently at her own expense, 'Too many late nights, me' implying that she does not look as well for her age as Shona does (Act 2, p. 60). She follows this up with the same query as Marlene and Win have used, but couched in more informal language: 'So what's the problem?' (Act 2, p. 60). Shona, like Jeanine, seems a little vague as to why she wants to move until Nell provides an explanation for her: 'You'd be interested in titular management status but not come off the road?' (Act 2, p. 60). In spite of her desire to find another tough bird in Shona, Nell challenges her claim that all of her calls are successful, and even when Shona concedes that a third are not, Nell continues to push the point: 'Because that's what an employer is going to have doubts about with a lady as I needn't tell you, whether she's got the guts to push through to a closing situation. They think we're too nice' (Act 2, p. 61). Her statement suggests that 'an employer' is likely to be a man, in spite of her own experience at Top Girls, and as a top salesperson. This may be a tactic to remind Shona of the harsh reality of life in the 'top fields', but it also suggests an unwillingness to believe anything can change: that women achievers will always be the exception rather than the rule.

CHECK THE BOOK

Sarah Daniels's *Masterpieces* was first produced at the Royal Exchange, Manchester, in 1983. It examines the difficulties faced by a range of working women – a teacher, a social worker and a secretary – in male-dominated workplaces. In particular the play analyses the effects of pornography on the treatment of women.

Even before Shona begins her speech, which embodies all the clichés of the 1980s success story peddled by magazines, films and advertisements during the decade, her hesitation is clear. Each time Nell asks her to elaborate on the information on her CV all she can say is that she likes driving and wants to be on the road. When asked to 'describe your present job' she once again echoes Nell's words before beginning her description: 'My present job at present' (Act 2, p. 63). The echoing and the redundant meanings it creates highlights her uncertainty and sets the tone for the rest of her speech; she seems to be repeating words she has heard before, and is not experienced enough to know how unlikely it is that someone in her position would be driving a Porsche, staying in hotels and eating steak every night. Her hunger for this lifestyle is palpable, but Churchill denies us any outcome that might indicate whether or not Shona will succeed. The scene peters out following her defiant 'I could though, I bet you' (Act 2, p. 63). As the humorous effect created by Shona's elaborate lies and Nell's exposing of them fades we are left wondering whether Shona will ever find a job.

PART THREE

CRITICAL APPROACHES

CHARACTERISATION

Churchill's rejection of **naturalism** (see also **Background: Literary background**) is reflected in the extent to which she experiments with the presentation and development of characters in her plays. Rather than displaying straightforward psychological development as, for example, Shakespeare does in *Macbeth*, where we see Macbeth move from a loyal servant, to a jealous rival, and finally to a power-crazed despot, Churchill's characters tend to a more **Brechtian** model of character development. One example of this is a tendency to express emotions through song (as in *Cloud Nine*, *Light Shining in Buckinghamshire* or *Serious Money*) or through their dramatic presentation. In *Owners* (1972) Churchill contrasts the acquisitive and active Marion with the passive, Zen-like Alec and in Act 1 of *Cloud Nine* (1979) the young Victoria is played by a doll in order to emphasise her passivity and idealised nature. In the original production, Joshua, the black servant, was played by a white actor to emphasise his subordination to the white family he serves and his internalisation of their values.

In *Top Girls*, Churchill juxtaposes characters from different social backgrounds and historical eras in order to demonstrate the diversity of womankind. Women are not just 'career girls' or wives, mothers, daughters and lovers, they are complex individuals and, as Act 1 demonstrates, they have always had to juggle their priorities in order to lead more fulfilling lives, and achieve a degree of satisfaction with their lot (even if, as in Gret's case, the only degree of satisfaction she achieves is avenging the tragic death of her children).

ACTIONING

In order to appreciate characterisation in *Top Girls* it helps to have an understanding of actioning, a technique developed by the play's first director, Max Stafford-Clark, which gives the actors a new way of exploring the motivations of their characters at every stage of the

 CHECK THE BOOK

In *Light Shining in Buckinghamshire* (1976) and *Cloud Nine* (1979) the same character is portrayed by different actors at different times. This emphasises the character's construction as a dramatic device, as well as commenting on the extent to which personality is itself constructed.

play, and which then guides them on how they might deliver their lines. Each actor goes through every line of their speech and assigns a verb summarising what they think their character is trying to achieve every time they speak. Deborah Findlay, who played Isabella, Mrs Kidd and Joyce in the 1982 and 1991 productions (filmed by the BBC), kept both her scripts, which show slightly different actions – a sign that the second production did not merely reconstruct the first. In discussing the difference between the first and second scripts she offers us both a way of reading the filmed performance and an insight into playing Joyce:

> When Marlene says 'come on Joyce, what a night,' we've got 'Marlene softens Joyce'. Then she 'praises' Joyce with the line 'you've got what it takes'. Joyce 'resists' all that, resists Marlene, with 'I know I have'. Marlene 'befriends' Joyce with 'I didn't really mean all that'. Joyce 'educates' Marlene with 'I did'.
>
> (Rabillard (ed.) (1998), p. 87)

The actioning words here are 'softens', 'praises', 'resists', 'befriends' and 'educates', and an examination of who does what to whom reveals that it is Joyce who holds the power in this exchange. Marlene's 'Come on Joyce, what a night' is designed to make Joyce feel sorry for Marlene and therefore to be kinder towards her, to make her feel softer towards her sister (Act 3, p. 87). By following this up with praise, 'You've got what it takes', she is hoping to make Joyce feel more kindly disposed to her, but Joyce can see through her attempts to make peace and so resists or rejects Marlene's compliment, saying 'I know I have' (Act 3, p. 87). This has the effect of making Marlene look patronising and so she tries to win Joyce over again by retracting everything she has said before in an attempt to make friends with ('befriend') Joyce. Joyce not only rejects this, she teaches Marlene that she cannot be easily pacified, and so she 'educates' her.

In the following section, the characters are discussed in the order they appear in the play.

 CHECK THE BOOK

Samples of Deborah Findlay's 1982 and 1991 scripts with actions noted are reproduced in Lizbeth Goodman's essay 'Overlapping Dialogue in Overlapping Media: Behind the Scenes of *Top Girls*', in Sheila Rabillard (ed.), *Essays on Caryl Churchill: Contemporary Representations* (1998).

 QUESTION

How would you 'action' the final scene between Joyce and Marlene?

MARLENE

Marlene is the play's central character. She embodies the aggressive 'me-first' philosophy that dominated business in the 1980s: 'I believe in the individual. Look at me' (Act 3, p. 84). She is a self-made woman who has sacrificed her child and her extended family in order to succeed in business. There is also a suggestion that she has sacrificed any kind of personal life. As Lizbeth Goodman notes in her introduction to the film version of *Top Girls*, Marlene appears to have no real friends to invite to her celebratory dinner, and, as she admits to Joyce, she cannot find a man to accept her as she is: they 'like to be seen with a high-flying lady. ... But they can't take the day to day. They're waiting for me to turn into the little woman' (Act 3, p. 83). In this respect she has much in common with Louise, the older woman interviewed by Win in Act 2, Scene 3, and with Nell, her young and ambitious colleague (see **The text: Extended commentaries 2 and 3** for more on these scenes).

Marlene grew up in a poor home and watched her mother suffer at her father's hands: 'She was hungry because he drank the money. / He used to hit her' (Act 3, p. 85). This experience left her determined not to repeat the same mistakes and so when she became pregnant she resolved to have an abortion. Her apparently infertile sister Joyce offered to adopt the child and bring it up as her own and Marlene accepted the offer and escaped to London where she became a successful career woman. She obviously feels some guilt at having abandoned her child – evidenced by the expensive presents she brings on her infrequent visits – and is aware of how much she owes Joyce, even though she finds it difficult to express it: 'You've been wonderful looking after Angie. ... I can't write letters but I do think of you' (Act 3, p. 82). When she offers Joyce financial support for looking after Angie she is trying to assuage her guilt at leaving them, but it also stems from a desire to offer practical support to them, and perhaps even to share her good fortune with the person who gave her the freedom to pursue her goals.

Two of the biggest questions the play raises are to what extent has Marlene aped male behaviour in order to achieve success, and to what extent do all successful women simply compound the problem

CHECK THE BOOK

Marlene's confidence is echoed by the strong female voice of Maya Angelou's anti-slavery poem 'Still I Rise': 'Does my sassiness upset you?' (*And Still I Rise*, 1978).

of female oppression by behaving like men. Critics are divided and often choose to highlight one aspect of Marlene's character at the expense of another. When reading the play it is important to remember that although she can be ruthless, Marlene can also be kind and is not entirely devoid of what is often seen as the traditional feminine impulse to nurture, as demonstrated by her concern to ensure that all her dinner guests' needs are attended to, and that they all get the chance to tell their stories. She has an easy relationship with her colleagues Win and Nell, taking their jokes about her late arrival in good part, 'Pass the sugar and shut your face, pet' (Act 2, p. 49); she is even polite to Mrs Kidd until she is accused of being masculine and unnatural (Act 2, p. 59). Her management strategy too sounds eminently reasonable: 'Naturally I'll be tactful and pleasant to him, you don't start pushing someone round. I'll consult him over any decisions affecting his department. But that's no different, Mrs Kidd, from any of my colleagues' (Act 2, p. 58).

Until Act 3, Marlene is also the most reticent and controlled character in the play. While she encourages all her guests to tell their stories in Act 1, she divulges almost nothing about herself, in spite of the fact that, like all her guests (except Isabella), she has lost a child and her father. Any information she does give is only in response to direct questions: she has a sister, but no dead lovers and has just become managing director of an employment agency. Her reply to Isabella's 'Do you have a sister?', 'Yes in fact', is an awkward grammatical construction that can be seen as reflecting both her awkward relationship with her sister and her awkwardness about talking about herself (Act 1, pp. 1–2). After Angie appears at the agency in Act 2, Nell asks Win, 'What's she got, brother, sister? She never talks about her family' (Act 2, p. 66). When she visits Joyce we see a less controlled side of Marlene, and a side of her that is uncomfortable with the fact that she is not in charge of events. She tries to play a number of different roles – the indulgent aunt, the city girl appreciating the fresh air, the long-lost sister nostalgic for the places of her childhood – but seems to be comfortable only when she is arguing with Joyce (interestingly, although Marlene is an assertive person, we never see Marlene behave in such a confrontational way in the rest of the play). Even then, after

 CHECK THE BOOK
In Charlotte Keatley's *My Mother Said I Never Should* (1987), Jackie gives up her child to her mother in order to make a success of her career, and, unlike Marlene, experiences continual guilt about her decision.

espousing her Thatcherite views on the working classes and people too 'stupid' and 'frightened' and 'lazy' to make a success of their lives, she is willing to backtrack for the sake of peace, telling Joyce, 'I didn't really mean all that' (Act 3, p. 87). Marlene is a complex character who embodies the struggle to reconcile traditional socialist feminism with material ambition.

ISABELLA BIRD

The real Isabella Bird's passion for travel and adventure made her an anomaly in her own time (reflected in the title of a biography of her, *A Curious Life for a Lady*), but, compared to the other dinner guests, she is socially conservative: a typical product of the Victorian era. She is the most conscious of good manners – distinct from Nijo's obsession with status – and tries to keep the party in order and to tone down any lewd or cruel remarks. (See **The text: Extended commentary 1** for more on Isabella's sense of social propriety.) This sense of propriety is reflected in her ambivalent attitude towards her sister, Hennie, whose acceptance of an uneventful and worthy life in 'the constant murk' makes her conscious of her selfishness in rejecting it (Act 1, p. 2). 'I can never be like Hennie. I was always so busy in England, a kind of business I detested' (Act 1, p. 25). This ambivalence can also be seen in her habit of referring to Hennie as 'its' rather than 'she' or 'her'. For every story she tells of her own liberation, she counters it with a sombre reflection on Hennie's goodness, or their father's or her own husband's kindness. Like Marlene, she feels guilty for abandoning her sister, but also, to some extent, she seems to feel guilty for enjoying herself – doing things for the sake of pleasure was frowned on in Victorian society.

The historical Isabella was devastated by Hennie's death and was nursed back to health by Dr John Bird (who had been regularly proposing to her since 1876). She married him in 1881, the year after Hennie's death, and devoted her life to him. When he became ill she nursed him until his death in 1886 and then returned to travelling, not for pleasure, but to visit medical missions. By 1890 she was already famous: she was made a fellow of the Royal Geographical Society in 1892 and gave a lecture there the same year – the first woman ever to do so. She had previously refused their invitations to

CHECK THE BOOK

Pat Barr's *A Curious Life for a Lady* (1970) is a study of Isabella's life.

QUESTION

Post-colonialism is a branch of cultural studies which seeks to reveal the attitudes towards colonies and 'colonials' or 'natives' expressed in works of literature, decorative arts and other cultural practices (such as museums). What post-colonial approaches do you think could be applied to *Top Girls*, specifically to the character of Isabella?

speak on the grounds that 'it seems scarcely consistent in a society which does not recognise the work of women to ask women to read a paper'.

Deborah Findlay, who played Churchill's fictional version of Isabella (and also Joyce) in the first production and in the 1991 revival at the Royal Court, said that for her Isabella's most important qualities were a sense of adventure and a sense of fun. Both of these are a challenge for an actor to convey at the dinner party when she is surrounded by more flamboyant, and less reticent, characters.

LADY NIJO

In the original production, Nijo was played by Lindsay Duncan, a tall, blonde, elegant and well-spoken actress. She made no attempt to disguise the fact that she was not Japanese, but her elegance and refined speaking voice will have contributed to the overall effect of Nijo as a fastidious and slightly vain person. Because of the highly ritualistic and hierarchical nature of the Japanese court, Nijo is obsessed with status and doing the right thing, and she makes frequent mention of the honours bestowed on her: 'When I was chosen to give sake to his Majesty's brother'; 'I had been publicly granted permission to wear thin silk' (Act 1, pp. 8, 12). This is one of the reasons for her distress (and uncharacteristically undignified behaviour) when the Emperor died and she was barred from the funeral: 'I hid in the room with his coffin, then I couldn't find where I'd left my shoes, I ran after the funeral procession in bare feet, I couldn't keep up' (Act 1, p. 26). Although she had a genuine affection for him, it is bound up with his status and hers: 'What I want to know is, if I'd still been at court, would I have been allowed to wear full mourning?' (Act 1, p. 26).

CHECK THE BOOK

The Methuen Student Edition of *Top Girls* has photographs from the first production in which Lindsay Duncan's make-up can be seen very clearly.

The swiftness of Nijo's emotional shifts, for example from reflecting on her distress at the death of her father and the Emperor, to wondering about her status, provide a number of comic interludes in the first act, but she should not be viewed as a shallow figure of fun. When Marlene tries to comfort her by assuring her that she is sure she would have been allowed to wear full mourning, Nijo rejects her attempts at consolation, showing some of the spirit that sustained her during the second half of her life. Her evident enjoyment of the finer things in life makes her renunciation of them even more impressive and suggests that she has a steelier core than she likes to show. Yet her willingness to follow her father's advice and 'enter holy orders' (Act 1, p. 3) also appeals because of her poetic and slightly melodramatic sensibility. It is likely that the audience would find many of her lines very funny as she applies a thirteenth-century Japanese understanding of life to the experiences of others, particularly when she suggests that Isabella might have written Rocky Mountain Jim a poem: 'Snow on the mountains. My sleeves are wet with tears' (Act 1, p. 9). (See **The text: Extended commentary 1** for more analysis of Nijo's character.)

DULL GRET

Gret is taciturn for the most part: she responds to questions with one-word answers, and her few comments are usually confined to the subject of food – 'Pig', 'Potatoes', 'Can we have some more bread?' (Act 1, pp. 4–5) – or sex. Her occasional interjections should therefore be studied carefully in order to see what motivates her and what her values are. She is clearly listening to the other guests as her remarks are always relevant, and often function as an echo or summation of the feelings being expressed by the group – most clearly illustrated when Nijo is talking of the depression she felt at leaving court, and Marlene, Joan and Isabella add their own accounts to hers. Joan remarks, 'You wish it [your life] was over', and Gret's response to this is 'Sad': the simplicity of the word (and the sound) punctuates the discussion as effectively as a full stop (Act 1, p. 7).

Her reticence makes her story the most affecting of all, as the words tumble over each other in her rush to get them out: 'We come into hell through a big mouth. Hell's black and red. / It's like the village where I come from' (Act 1, p. 27). Her choice of 'come' rather than 'came' suggests the immediacy of the experience – she is reliving it as she tells the guests. It is also a departure from formal grammar in keeping with her background as peasant (she would not be able to read or write). Her social circumstances make it unlikely that she would have much to contribute to the wider discussions of religion and courtly tradition, but the actor playing the part could make

www. CHECK THE NET

The Asia Department of the Victoria and Albert Museum has several prints of the Tale of Genji, a noblewoman like Nijo, who also wrote about her life. Go to **www.vam.ac.uk**, click on 'Search the Collections' and enter 'Genji' to see the prints and read the story of Lady Genji.

www. CHECK THE NET

The Museum Mayer van den Bergh in Antwerp holds the painting in which Dull Gret is featured. It was painted by Pieter Brueghel the Elder between 1561 and 1562. The museum website has an image of the picture and further information about it. Go to **http://museum.antwerpen.be/mayervandenbergh**, select Collection 'Dulle Griet' ('Mad Meg' in English).

QUESTION

Does Gret's behaviour make her a comic figure? How does her tragic story change your perception of her character?

CHECK THE POEM

'Pope Joan' by Carol Ann Duffy is one of the poems in *The World's Wife* (1999), a volume re-imagining the lives of mythical and historical women. Duffy's Joan is reminded of her own humanity by the experience of childbirth: 'the closest I felt/ to the power of God/ was the sense of a hand/ lifting me, flinging me down,/ lifting me/ flinging me down,/ as my baby pushed out between my legs' (*The World's Wife*, p. 68).

much of showing her lack of interest in these subjects, or of showing that she is overawed by the restaurant and other guests.

In production Gret's lack of speech tends to be countered by her activity at the table. In all three productions discussed below (see **Critical approaches: Staging**) she steals food and other items from the table: crockery, cutlery, bottles and anything else she can lay her hands on.

POPE JOAN

As with all the characters in the restaurant scene, Joan's is a mixture of comedy and **pathos**. Her character is open to a variety of interpretations by different actors and readers: she might be very aloof at the beginning and become progressively more intimate as she gets drunk. (Joan's drunkenness is indicated in Churchill's stage directions: first she notes that '*They are quite drunk. They get the giggles*' (Act 1, p. 19) and then at the end of the act, '*JOAN gets up and is sick in a corner*' (Act 1, p. 29)). She might also be played as an absent minded and socially inept intellectual. At points she certainly seems unaware of how different she is, for example, when she first arrives, and Marlene tries to introduce her naturally into the conversation by asking her, 'What excited you when you were ten?' Her response, 'Because angels are without matter they are not individuals. Every angel is a species' (Act 1, p. 4), is hardly conventional dinner-party small talk and Marlene has to make a joke to cover the awkward silence ('There you are'). Or a director might choose to emphasise the way in which she vacillates between anguish about her blasphemous role, 'Unfortunately there were earthquakes, and some village reported it had rained blood, and in France there was a plague of giant grasshoppers, but I don't think that can have been my fault, do you?', and anger at the structures which prevented her from following the same career path as a woman, 'Women, children and lunatics can't be Pope' (Act 1, p. 14, 15). There is more about Joan in **The text: Extended commentary 1**.

GRISELDA

Griselda is as meek and submissive in the restaurant scene as she is in the works of literature that celebrate her. She is apologetic about arriving late and shrinks from Marlene's attempts to order a meal for her, sticking to cheese and biscuits while everyone else orders luxurious desserts. Because she turns up late, she is also much more sober than the other guests which might be one of the reasons that she is so defensive of her husband's appalling behaviour towards her. Lesley Manville, who played Griselda in the original production of the play at the Royal Court, had great difficulty in accepting Griselda's passivity (particularly in comparison to the other strong women present at the dinner party). She also suggested that: 'it's significant that she arrives late in that scene, because what debate could you have with her? She can only tell her story, she's not movable at all' (Goodman in Rabillard (1998), p. 74). Griselda is the only character in the first act who never chose her own course of action, she always obeyed men: first her father, and then her husband. Her reputation is fixed for ever as the good and patient Griselda, and, as shocking as her husband's treatment of her was, she is also the only guest present who appears happy and content, except for the tantalising moment when she muses (almost to herself), 'I do think – I do wonder – it would have been nicer if Walter hadn't had to' (Act 1, p. 27). Because Griselda (the literary character) was created in order to demonstrate the adage that 'virtue (in this case obedience) is its own reward' she gets the contentment that the other women are denied.

CHECK THE BOOK
'The Clerk's Tale' from Chaucer's *The Canterbury Tales* is the longest rendition of Griselda's story.

JOYCE

Joyce is a difficult character to analyse, perhaps the most difficult in the play. Like Marlene, she is a complex character, who has suffered and made sacrifices in the pursuit of happiness, but for both of them it is questionable how much happiness they have achieved. Where Marlene nearly always presents a polished and pleasant façade, Joyce is mercurial: angry and unfriendly one minute, then loving and indulgent the next, particularly with Angie. This is most obvious in Act 2, Scene 2 when she tries to entice Angie back into the house with the offer of tea and chocolate biscuits and then swears at her when she does not respond (see **The text: Detailed summaries** for a deeper analysis of this moment). In Act 3, this manifests itself most clearly at the beginning of the action when she is trying to simultaneously indulge Angie's delight at being given presents – to the extent that she lets Angie open her presents from Marlene too ('Yes, you open it pet', Act 3, p. 67) – and keep her under control by reminding her to go upstairs to change into her dress. Similarly, she speaks of her husband's infidelity and their subsequent separation dispassionately, but then fondly recalls that he was 'lovely' when they were first engaged (Act 3, p. 82).

Joyce, Marlene and Angie are the only characters who have an opportunity to develop over the course of the play. All the others appear only in either Act 1 or Act 2 and so their development is limited to a particular period of time. All three of them develop most significantly during the third act, on home ground.

CHECK THE FILM

Billy Elliot (2001), directed by Steven Daldry, tells the story of a boy from a working-class mining community who becomes a ballet dancer. The evocation of Britain in the 1980s is a useful analogy to the kind of life Joyce might lead.

When we first encounter Joyce and Angie (in Act 2, Scene 2), we have no idea whether or not Angie has a valid reason for hating her mother and wanting to hide from her. Joyce's behaviour when Angie refuses to come in the second time she is called – swearing at her daughter and threatening to lock her out – suggests that Angie is entirely justified in her hatred. It is only in Act 3 that Joyce's resentment of Angie is explained: both by Angie's odd behaviour and by the revelation that Angie's hyperactiveness caused Joyce to miscarry her own child.

The differences between the two sisters are clearly longstanding ones. The childhood that turned Marlene into a capitalist has confirmed Joyce as a socialist. She espouses the socialist values of universal brotherhood and equality for all and her anger is a result of seeing these values discarded in the pursuit of wealth. Yet, for all her political leanings, Joyce is much harder than Marlene, and could be seen as much more unforgiving. As their argument escalates she warns Marlene, 'don't be round here when it [the revolution against capitalism] happens because if someone's kicking you I'll just laugh' (Act 3, p. 86). Even if this is just socialist rhetoric, it is still an unpleasant thing to say to someone. She also rejects all of Marlene's attempts to make amends: her offer of money, her clumsy gestures of thanks – 'You've been wonderful looking after Angie ... I can't write letters but I do think of you' (Act 3, p. 82) – and even her attempt to be friends. The message seems to be that whether women choose a career (as Marlene does) or a family (as Joyce does) they still end up alone and divided from each other.

QUESTION

Is Joyce a victim of a society that does not value women who seek to bring up their children, or a rebel who has chosen to reject society's emphasis on individual success?

ANGIE

Angie's motivations are usually very obvious: she wants to scare Kit and to befriend her; to charm Marlene and impress her; and to 'kill' her adoptive mother. However, the way in which she goes about trying to achieve these actions is doomed to failure. She does frighten Kit, but that jeopardises their friendship; her attempts to charm Marlene just alarm her; and she never kills her mother (or rather adoptive mother).

She has inherited her real mother's ambition and determination (she succeeds in getting to London and finding the employment agency), and her desire for a better lifestyle ('I want to go to America. Will you take me?', Act 3, p. 75), but it seems unlikely that she will ever master the other skills needed to succeed. In this way she is reminiscent of Jeanine and Shona, the two young women interviewed in Act 2, who want to live the 'top girl' life, but are unlikely to get the opportunities. She is just another of the young women that society has written off, although the part played in this by her learning difficulties is hard to infer from the text. Joyce tells Marlene that Angie has been in remedial classes for the last two years, but also that Angie is always reading and cutting things about politicians out of the newspapers (Act 3, p. 77) which suggests that her difficulties are behavioural. Her conduct in Act 2 would seem to confirm this: not only in the way that she tries to bully Kit, but also because of the difficulty she has in relating to new people when she gets to the Top Girls Employment Agency.

> **CONTEXT**
>
> Joyce's pessimism about Angie's prospect of employment is justified: by 1981, 2.7 million people were unemployed.

KIT

Although she has a relatively small part, Kit has a pivotal role in the play as another example of womanhood in the future. Clever and confident (as she tells Joyce, 'I could [be a nuclear physicist], I'm clever'), her quick intelligence and maturity act as a foil to Angie's immaturity and childlike fixation with her aunt and with gore (Act 2, p. 43). Her ability to project herself beyond her immediate surroundings (a sign of maturity) is demonstrated by the contrast between Angie's attempts to frighten her with stories of ghostly kittens and poltergeists while Kit is genuinely haunted by the possibility of a nuclear war. Her desire to be a nuclear scientist shows a rational desire to control her fear by understanding more

CHECK THE FILM

The BBC film *Threads* (1984) shows the impact of nuclear war on Sheffield. The film was shown in many schools in Britain in the 1980s and could be the catalyst for Kit's fears.

about it, as well as showing a degree of awareness of current affairs and an ability to live in the present moment rather than in a fantasy world (as Angie does).

Kit has also learned how to exert power over Angie, despite being younger and physically weaker. She knows that Angie is sensitive about her outcast status with her peers, and taunts her with it when she has had enough of Angie's bullying: 'My mother says there's something wrong with you playing with someone my age. She says why haven't you got friends of your own age. People your own age know there's something funny about you' (Act 2, p. 39).

Kit's brief appearance in Act 3 allows us to realise how much she has matured in the intervening year: when she is introduced to Marlene in Act 3, she barely acknowledges her existence and focuses all her attention on Angie, which suggests that she is both shy and lacking in manners. A year later (in Act 2) she seems much more confident and mature, and this helps to point up how little change there has been in Angie.

WIN

Like Marlene, Win has paid a huge price for her professional success: in many ways she would not be out of place in Act 1, sharing the story of her tumultuous journey to the peak of her profession. She gave up an academic career doing medical research because 'there's no money in it', and, like many of her historical counterparts in Act 1, decided to go abroad to find fulfilment (Act 2, p. 65). Although she enjoyed America – 'Americans know how to live' – and found the work easy, she still ended up having a nervous breakdown: 'thought I was five different people' (Act 2, p. 65). Like Marlene she has tolerated a string of unsatisfactory relationships in preference to being alone, and is currently engaged in an affair with a married man (she is also married – to a man in prison). It is significant that we find all this out after she has interviewed Louise so sensitively. We begin to understand that she and the other 'top girls' all fear ending up like Louise.

Her confession to Angie reveals yet another facet of her character. She tells her, 'Any job I ever did I started doing it better than the rest of the crowd and they didn't like it' (Act 2, p. 65), which suggests that she is highly competitive and not particularly modest – factors which have probably contributed to her successful career at the Top Girls Agency. Her toughness of character can also be seen in her response to the news of Howard's heart attack (as discussed in **The text: Detailed summaries**). (See also **The text: Extended commentary 2** for more analysis of Win's character.)

NELL

Like Win, the actor playing Nell has a very short space of time in the play in which to establish her character. She is keen and ambitious – as demonstrated by the fact that she applied for the managing director's job – and extremely conscious of the image she wants to project, which is competent and dynamic: 'I've never been a staying put lady' (Act 2, p. 46). When Win comments that she should not be wasting her time on an old salesman, Nell retorts, 'I don't waste a lot' (Act 2, p. 47). This line might be delivered sharply, as if to rebuke Win for the suggestion, or it might be delivered in a humorous way, as if to prove that she can afford the odd act of kindness. The relationship between Nell and Win as a whole could be realised so that they either appear to be genuinely friendly, or that they are just pretending to be friends in order to keep tabs on each other. (see **The text: Extended commentary 3** for more analysis of Nell's character.)

STRUCTURE

In common with many modern plays, *Top Girls* disregards the Aristotelian unities of time, space and action, in order to explore the impact of the modern world on the lives of women. Several critics of the first production remarked that the play is really a series of one-act plays, or as Sheridan Morley put it: '*Top Girls* is essentially not one but three excellent short plays' (Morley (1983), p. 349). There are three acts, each of which examines the plight of different groups of women. The action takes place in three separate locations (a restaurant, the Top Girls Employment Agency and Joyce's home) and covers episodes over the course of a year in the lives of Marlene, Angie and Joyce, but presents them in reverse chronological order –

> **CONTEXT**
>
> According to Aristotle's principles of dramatic composition, the *unity of action* assumes that a play should have one main action that it follows, with few or no sub-plots. The *unity of place* assumes a play should cover a single physical space and should not attempt to compress geography, or represent more than one place. The *unity of time* assumes the action in a play will take place over no more than twenty-four hours.

CHECK THE BOOK

J. L. Styan's *Modern Drama in Theory and Practice: Realism and Naturalism* (1981) provides a lengthy and detailed account of the development of **realism** and **naturalism** in theatre.

and in doing so defies the structure of the naturalistic play in which action and consequence are carefully plotted to allow the audience to anticipate the outcome of the play and to provide a moral homily.

Top Girls begins with a digression. Marlene, the main character, is, and is not, the focus of the first act. She is the host of a party to celebrate her promotion, but it is her guests who relate the stories of their lives and who are the focus of our attention. There is no resolution to the act and no indication that this is the last we will see of the historical procession of 'top girls'. By beginning the play in a period which is simultaneously bound by history (the style of the restaurant, the gathering of a group of unchaperoned women in it and Marlene's ability to become managing director are twentieth-century phenomena) and freed from historical constraints and the conventions of realistic drama (the gathering of women from the seventh to twentieth centuries in the same place at the same time) allows the audience to appreciate the long and circuitous course of women's liberation.

QUESTION

What effects does the disjointed timeframe create? Would the play seem more optimistic if the action were presented in a chronological sequence, and ended on Marlene's pronouncement on Angie: 'She's not going to make it' (p. 66)?

Act 2 encompasses the worlds of Marlene and Joyce, moving between the commercial world of the Top Girls Employment Agency and the domestic setting of Joyce's home and backyard. They are worlds apart from each other geographically, socially and economically but linked by Angie (who appears in both). The action begins at the Agency, moves to Joyce's East Anglian home, and then back to the Agency, and takes place over an unspecified period of time. We have no idea how long it took Angie to come to London after she declared her intentions to Kit, and there is no indication how long it is since the dinner party. In Scene 3, Win and Nell offer their congratulations to Marlene, who seems to have a hangover ('Mind my head', p. 49), which suggests the dinner party may have been the previous night, but we have no way of verifying this.

The stage directions and the state of Angie's dress inform us that Act 3 takes place a year earlier (the first concrete indicator of time) allowing us to see the consequences of Marlene's actions in reverse order: we see Marlene's life and Angie's appearance in it before we know the connection between them.

LANGUAGE AND STYLE

OVERLAPPING DIALOGUE

Although it is not the first play to use overlapping dialogue, or even the first of Churchill's plays to employ the technique, *Top Girls* is renowned for the way in which conversations are structured to overlap. In the first scene in particular, most critics have interpreted this as an indication of the women's competitive and self-absorbed natures, but a close analysis of their turn-taking patterns reveals that the women's overlapping speech actually tends to support the other's speaker's story, rather than trying to begin a new story. In the exchange below the women's speech is cooperative rather than competitive; it is also closer to how conversation works in real life (people seldom wait for someone else to finish before responding):

MARLENE: Were your travels just a penance? Avocado
                vinaigrette. Didn't you / enjoy yourself?
JOAN: Nothing to start with for me, thank you.
NIJO: Yes, but I was very unhappy. / It hurts to
                remember
MARLENE: And the wine list.
NIJO: the past. I think that was repentance.
MARLENE: Well I wonder.
NIJO: I might just have been homesick.
MARLENE: Or angry.
NIJO: Not angry, no, / why angry?

(Act 1, p. 5)

On the page it is clear that the women are all following the same conversational thread (Nijo's experiences as a nun), but are also ordering their food. Churchill omits the stage direction in each speech that would read ('*to the waitress*'), so on this occasion, they are not interrupting each other, they are turning away to speak to someone else, in fact performing two tasks at once. (See **The text: Extended commentaries 2 and 3** for more on turn-taking and politeness theory.)

CHECK THE BOOK
At the same time as Churchill was writing *Top Girls* linguists were challenging assumptions about the differences between the speech of men and women, for example: that women talk more than men, use more **euphemisms** and intensifiers, and are more polite. See Deborah Cameron's *Feminism and Linguistic Theory* (1985) for more on feminist linguistics.

NAMING

One of the aims of the Women's Liberation Movement in the 1970s and 1980s was to change the terminology used about women: in particular to stop people using derogatory or infantilising terms about them (bird, girl, baby, sweetie). In *Top Girls*, the terms people use to refer to themselves and each other reveal a great deal about their opinions of each other, and themselves. Marlene habitually uses 'pet' (a dialect word) as a term of endearment to her colleagues and her dinner guests. Joyce also calls Angie and Marlene 'pet' in Act 3. It echoes Isabella's references to Hennie as 'my own pet' (Act 1, p. 2), reinforcing the link between Marlene and Isabella. Win and Nell refer to each other and Marlene as 'ladies', and for them it is a term of approval. They use 'bird' in the same way; Win tells Angie, 'Your aunty's a smashing bird' (Act 3, p. 64).

The way Win and Nell talk about Shona indicates how high their opinion is of her. Nell announces, 'I've a lady here thinks she can sell', to which Win replies, 'Tough bird like us' (Act 1, p. 48). Louise, who thinks like a man and is hostile towards other women in the workplace, answers Win's question, 'Are you the only woman?', with 'Apart from the girls, of course yes.' This would raise a laugh in the theatre for two reasons: first the seemingly illogical nature of her answer ('girl' and 'woman' both refer to females), but also because it reveals her lack of respect for the other women she works with. The 'girls' are presumably her junior in age and status, as she refers to the one female assistant she had as 'a young woman' (Act 1, p. 52).

SPEECH STYLES

Each of the characters in the play has her own distinctive speech style (just as people do in real life) and these speech styles help us place the characters geographically and socially. Both Gret and Angie, who are the least educated women in the play, have a very limited vocabulary, tend to speak in simple sentences and use grammatical formulations which are not found in formal **standard English** (in their confusion of past and present tenses for example). Shona, whose educational level is unknown, is inarticulate for the most part, stumbling over her answers, and repeating the question she has just been asked, which puts her on a level with Gret and Angie. However, when she launches into her flight of fantasy (which sounds as if it has been taken straight from the pages of a magazine or film), she speaks with confidence, although the predominance of short sentences and repeated words is an indication of her relatively low level of linguistic fluency: '*Big* ones with *big freezers. Big freezers.* And *I stay in hotels* at night when I'm away from home. On my expense account. I *stay in various hotels*' (Act 2, p. 63).

The most articulate characters tend to be the best educated and the highest on the social scale: by adoption (in the case of Marlene and Griselda); by birth (in the case of Isabella and Nijo); or by education (in the case of Win and Joan). They have recourse to a larger vocabulary and explore abstract ideas but still tend to use relatively short sentences – particularly in Act 1 – in order to make it easier for the actor to time the overlapping speeches. Isabella's account of her own marriage is a good example of this: 'I did wish marriage had seemed more of a step. I tried very hard to cope with the ordinary drudgery of life. I was ill with carbuncles on the spine and nervous prostration' (Act 1, p. 11).

Despite the use of some unfamiliar vocabulary ('drudgery', 'carbuncles' and 'prostration'), which is as much an indication of Isabella's historical period as it is of her class, she keeps to a simple sentence structure so that the others can weave their own speeches in and out of the main conversational thread.

Another notable linguistic feature of the play is the modern jargon used by Marlene, Win and Nell. They have a kind of shorthand they use to denote approval. For example, when Joan is describing the Rogation Day procession, Marlene comments, 'Total Pope', presumably to convey her admiration for the power that Joan wielded and the spectacle it produced (Act 1, p. 17). Similarly, Win and Nell talk about being 'ace' at 'playing house' – meaning that they would do it very well (Act 2, p. 48).

 CHECK THE BOOK
The Feminist Critique of Language, edited by Deborah Cameron (1998), is a collection of extracts and articles exploring theories and concepts about the way in which men and women speak.

THEMES

POLITICS

Politics are all important to the study of *Top Girls*, even though there is no overt discussion of them until the end of the play. At the time it was written, Britain was going through a major political shift from broad cross-party agreement on the need for state support of industry, the health service, affordable housing and free education (in place since the Second World War) to a competitive market environment where people, businesses and institutions would be encouraged to become self-sufficient. Joyce and Marlene represent the two different political positions, with Marlene supporting competition and Joyce supporting collective responsibility. It would have been apparent to most British people who saw or read the play in the early 1980s that Marlene is in sympathy with Margaret Thatcher – even before she tells Joyce she '[c]ertainly gets my vote' (Act 3, p. 84). Similarly, most people would have appreciated that, until Act 3, the play appears to be a celebration of Thatcherite values and of the progress made towards female equality, a feeling that is shattered by Joyce's passionate articulation of the gulf which is opening up between those who 'have' and those who 'have not'.

The differences between Marlene and Joyce are revealed to have a long historical basis, which parallels the party-political division. Marlene argues for the particular, echoing the Right-wing emphasis on the individual, claiming that Thatcher's victory and the victories of individual women like her are a sign of progress. Joyce argues for the collective Left-wing view, explaining their father's violence towards their mother as a symptom of the degrading nature of capitalist oppression: 'Working in the fields like an animal. Why wouldn't he want a drink?' (Act 3, p. 84). (See **Background: Historical background** for more about the politics of the 1980s.)

FEMINISM

The birth of the Women's Liberation Movement in 1970 spawned an entire academic discipline (Women's Studies) and an interest in women marginalised in previous accounts of history, science, literature and other areas of cultural production. Indeed, the first

Women's Liberation Conference was held at Ruskin College, Oxford, because the feminist historians who belonged to the History Workshop Movement there had argued for a broadening out of the Workshop's focus from the contribution of the working class to include the contribution of women to history. Two publishers, Virago and the Women's Press, were set up to rediscover lost works by women as well as publishing new ones; many women (including Churchill) began to write plays about famous historical women, all in order to demonstrate the worth of women to society and the need to redress inequalities towards them. There was also a great rediscovery of women's diaries, letters and autobiographies (like those of Isabella and Nijo) and plays, poems and novels written detailing women's domestic lives.

> **CONTEXT**
>
> The Women's Liberation Movement was linked to the Gay Liberation front. Both followed the model of the Black Civil Rights Movement in the USA in terms of reclaiming their history from the margins of society.

Top Girls combines all these different aspects to produce a play which focuses on women in the public sphere rather than the domestic one (although this is where the play finishes). Churchill has spoken many times about the various inspirations for *Top Girls*: 'the idea of a load of dead women having coffee with someone from the present'; 'an idea about women doing all kinds of jobs'; Thatcher becoming Prime Minister; and Churchill's encounters with feminists in the USA for whom feminism was detached from left-wing politics:

> They were saying things were going very well: they were getting far more women executives, women vice-presidents and so on. And that was such a different attitude from anything I'd ever met here [Britain], where feminism tends to be much more connected to socialism and not so much to do with women succeeding on the sort of capitalist ladder.
>
> (Churchill interviewed by Lynne Truss,
> *Plays and Players* (February 1983))

Margaret Thatcher, who became Prime Minister in the same year as Churchill write *Cloud Nine*, fitted very much into this American line of feminism. *Top Girls* can be seen as Churchill's attempt to explore her own confusion at the conflation of capitalism and feminism, encapsulated in Joyce's question, 'What good's first woman if it's her?' (Act 3, p. 84). The play asks many questions about feminism. What happens to the collective basis on which feminism is built if the only way for women to succeed is to behave like men? What happens when someone like Marlene becomes a role-model for other women, as she is for Win, Nell, Angie and Shona?

MARRIAGE

Marriage is not a state that any of the characters in the play aspire to: even Griselda marries only because it is her duty to obey the Marquis and she would 'rather obey the Marquis than a boy from the village' (Act 1, p. 21). For all the historical characters in the play marriage is a gamble, a transaction that shifts them from the possession of their father to another man, rather than a love-match. In reality, for some women, the control of a husband might be preferable to the control of a father; for others, it might be worse. Some fathers and husbands did treat their daughters and wives as equals in any case, although law and tradition did not oblige them to do so. In addition, the very wealthy or widowed also had the opportunity to live independent lives. Another alternative was to enter holy orders, as Nijo did. Female emancipation was also partly a matter of economics: unless a family was wealthy they would be unlikely to be able to support one unmarried daughter, let alone more than one, and there were very few jobs open to 'respectable' women in the middle classes until the twentieth century.

This situation improved in the early twentieth century. People did begin to marry for love, and women tended to have at least some say in who their partner would be. Isabella marries out of gratitude (her husband nursed her sister, Hennie, until her death), but her marriage is one between equals, as we discover from her comments during Griselda's tale: 'I swore to obey dear John, of course, but it didn't seem to arise' (Act 1, p. 21) and, 'My poor John, I never loved him enough, and he would never have dreamt' (Act 1, p. 24).

In contrast, Joyce's marriage was clearly not an equal partnership. Although she 'fancied him. For about three years', her marriage did not turn out to be so different from that of her mother and father (Act 3, p. 83). She stayed at home and looked after Angie and the house while Frank went to work and had affairs with other women:

CHECK THE BOOK

One of the only jobs open to respectable middle-class women in the nineteenth century was that of governess. Charlotte Brontë's *Jane Eyre* (1847) examines the mingled feelings this job created in women: relief at achieving a degree of financial independence mixed with humiliation at being a servant.

'and if I wanted to go out in the evening he'd go mad, even if it was nothing, an evening class' (Act 3, p. 82).

Marlene cannot find anyone to respect her as an equal: men are attracted by her success but expect her to give it up and become a housewife. Win and Nell are also suspicious of marriage. Win is having an affair with a married man and enjoys pretending that they live together when his wife is away. She is also married (something she did 'in a moment of weakness') to a man in prison and given that she never goes to see him and is having an affair with someone else, it seems unlikely that their marriage will last (Act 3, p. 65). Nell, like Marlene, has had plenty of offers, but is not prepared to sacrifice her career in order to 'play house'. Jeanine's intention to get married is one of the things that convinces Marlene that she will never make it as a 'top girl'. In fact, the only person for whom marriage is presented as an attractive option is Angie. For all Joyce's own independence, she suggests to Kit and Marlene that Angie's only chance of a decent future is to marry: 'She's not going to get a job when jobs are hard to get. ... She'd better get married' (Act 2, p. 43). On the whole marriage is not presented as an attractive option in the world of the play.

CHECK THE NET
The BBC website has a page of personal memories of the 1980s in Britain, with topics such as money, Thatcher and recession. Go to **www.bbc.co.uk** and search for '1980s' and click on 'The 1980s – World Events'.

MOTHERHOOD

It is tempting to say that there are no role models for motherhood in *Top Girls*: Marlene, Nijo and Griselda willingly abandon their children; Gret and Joan are unable to save them from death; and Joyce swears at Angie and criticises her continually (albeit because she worries about her future). This might be explained by the play's focus on women beyond the domestic realm. The guests at the dinner party have not been invited because they are mothers. They have been invited because of the remarkable things they have done: Isabella's and Nijo's travels and literary contributions; Gret's courageous stand against evil; Joan's reign as Pope; Griselda's dumb obedience in the face of horrifying abuse.

Motherhood is a complex area in the play, reflecting changing attitudes towards the role of women both in modern Britain and throughout history. Although feminism challenges the notion that there are innate qualities belonging to each sex (as discussed in **The** text: Detailed summaries, Act 1) and rejects the notion that maternal feelings are one of these innate qualities in women – it is still a fact of nature that only women can give birth to children. This does not mean that they must, or that, having done so, they have a stronger nurturing instinct than men do, but, because there is still inequality in the amount men and women are paid, it is more usual for mothers to give up work, or reduce their hours, than it is for men to do so, thus reinforcing the idea of an innate maternal streak. Marlene's apparent absence of this streak (and apparent lack of children) is touched on by Mrs Kidd, who labels her 'unnatural', when in fact, like Nijo, Marlene believed she was being pragmatic. Marlene is prepared to entertain the notion of motherhood (however fleetingly) once she has achieved success (thus she is prepared to take Angie on in Act 3 – although the sincerity of this offer is difficult to assess), but was not prepared to do so when she was younger.

DRAMATIC TECHNIQUES

ALIENATION

CONTEXT

Bertolt Brecht (1898–1956) was a German playwright, director and poet whose work and techniques have had a huge effect on western drama. Brecht used theatre as a tool to educate his audiences and to shake them out of their complacency. He believed that plays should not confirm people's thoughts and prejudices but should cause them to question them.

Alienation, or *Verfremdungseffekt*, is the term Bertolt Brecht coined to describe the process of continually reminding people that they are watching a play. He wanted the audience to reflect critically on the action presented in the play and the questions it raised, rather than this being lost by their identification with, sympathy or hostility towards the characters involved. He used various techniques for doing this: placards stating the time and place of the action and summarising the action of the scene; cartoons, film and masks; and having actors comment on the scenes they are playing in. This style of acting is completely at odds with the Stanislavskyian system which dominated the **naturalist** tradition in which actors sought to identify and totally immerse themselves in their characters.

Using adults to play children is another example of alienation. It is impossible to forget that you are watching actors playing characters when adults are dressed in children's clothes. Churchill had used this device to great effect in *Cloud Nine* (1979): the actors are not only adults in children's costumes (in this case a sailor suit and a frilly dress), they are also cross-gendered. So a woman plays a boy dressed in a sailor suit and a man plays a girl wearing a dress. In *Top Girls*, she reuses this technique, having Angie and Kit played by adults while engaging in childish pursuits. The gathering together of the historic women is another example of alienation as it immediately reminds us that we are watching a theatrical event.

DOUBLING

Doubling refers to the long established theatrical practice of using the same actors to play two or more parts. Its use is often explained by economics (a small company means a small wage bill), but sometimes it serves a wider purpose, drawing parallels between characters played by the same actor. There are sixteen characters in *Top Girls*, one of whom never speaks (the waitress). Churchill has been quoted saying that she wrote the play as if a different actress would play each role:

> When it came to doing it, partly because it was being directed by Max Stafford-Clark who is in Joint Stock anyway and is used to working and likes working in that way, partly financial considerations (I mean no one's going to want to do a play with 16 actors when they can economise and do it with 7) and partly because it is obviously much more enjoyable for the actors and the whole *feel* of a play for it to be done by a company – it did seem to make a lot of sense to do it in that way.
>
> (Churchill, *Plays and Players* (January 1983), p. 10)

Churchill, the actors from the 1991 production and Stafford-Clark all play down the significance of the doubling, but in performance, and even on close reading, there are some very clear parallels between the characters. Pope Joan, who lived as a man and had 'nothing in my life except for my studies' is played by the same actor who later plays Louise, who likes to 'think I pass as a man at work' (Act 1, p. 12; Act 2, p. 52). Dull Gret becomes 'dull' Angie, another woman who has difficulty communicating, comes from a poor background and faces an uncertain future. The silent waitress from Act 1 becomes Kit – which in performance might suggest that Kit's confidence in her future as a nuclear physicist may be

CHECK THE BOOK

Brecht's *On Theatre*, translated by John Willet (1978), contains all of Brecht's best known writings on the theatre, including his explanations of alienation.

CONTEXT

Konstantin Stanislavsky (1863–1938) was a Russian actor, director and teacher who created the most influential acting system in the western world. He advocated total psychological immersion in a role combined with a precise vocal technique and physical gestures as the best means of realising the 'truth' of the character in production. His system is the basis for the Method acting style.

QUESTION

What inferences can you draw by examining the original allocation of roles in *Top Girls* (reprinted in full in the Methuen Student Edition)? Could the characters be doubled in any other way? For example, could Griselda and Joyce be played by the same actor, and how would it change your view of their characters?

misplaced and that, in fact, waitressing may be the career awaiting her. The same actress also plays Shona, the fantasist Nell interviews in Act 2, Scene 3, which offers the further possibility that Kit's confidence in her abilities is as misplaced as Shona's. In *Light Shining in Buckinghamshire* (1976) and *Cloud Nine* (1979) Churchill experimented with doubling as a further form of alienation. In *Light Shining in Buckinghamshire* a character was not always played by the same actor, disrupting any possibilities of the audience sympathising with the character without acknowledging that they were watching a performance. In *Cloud Nine*, the actors swapped parts between Acts 1 and 2 to reinforce the message that gender and sexuality are constructed and performed rather than innate. So Vicky, played by a doll in Act 1, is played by a man in Act 2; Betty, played by a man in Act 1 to emphasise the fact that she is entirely a man's creation, becomes a woman in Act 2 as she discovers her independence.

STAGING

CONTEXT

Proscenium arch theatres – in which the entire stage is behind the arch – were first introduced in the nineteenth century and were designed for **naturalistic** 'fourth wall' dramas.

Top Girls was first performed at the Royal Court Theatre, a proscenium arch or 'picture frame' theatre, where the stage is at one end of the room and the audience all sit in front of it . However, the style of the play is such that it could be performed in the round, on a thrust stage, or in any kind of space. The script does not contain many stage directions specifying how the stage business (or action) should be carried out; they simply indicate that certain effects must be achieved (for example, eating and drinking in Acts 1 and 3, making coffee at the beginning of Act 2). The set might be fully realised so that, in the office scenes, for example, there would be desks, chairs, filing cabinets, telephones, lamps, a coffee machine and all the other equipment you might find in an office in the 1980s (although a computer would probably not be part of it). Or it could be suggested very simply by a variety of tables and chairs which could be used for the restaurant scene, then for the office scenes, then to build a shelter for Kit and Angie, and finally for Joyce's kitchen table.

THE FIRST PRODUCTION

Every production of a play, and every performance, will be slightly different and it is important to remember that the published script may differ from the play as it was first performed, sometimes very substantially, in other cases in small, but important ways. One example of this in *Top Girls* is in Act 1 when Pope Joan is remembering her rise to the top and Marlene says: 'Yes, success is very ...' and leaves the line unfinished (Act 1, p. 12). This is a very important moment: Marlene's hesitation and inability, or unwillingness, to finish the sentence suggests that perhaps success is not as important to her as she thought it would be. Or, it could be taken as a sign that success is so marvellous that she cannot find the words to describe it, or simply that Joan continues to talk over her and so she does not bother to end the sentence. In the original production, however, Churchill provided an ending for the line when questioned by the actors:

> At some point in rehearsal they wanted me to complete it. They said, 'what would she have said?' and I said, 'alarming'. But it was actually meant to be an unfinished line and it's one of the things I'm correcting back. It seems more appropriate that Marlene doesn't quite manage to find what she thinks about success.
>
> (Churchill, *Plays and Players* (January 1983), p. 8)

Ending the line with 'alarming' might suggest that Marlene is not as confident as she appears: a suggestion that could be interpreted as anti-feminist (i.e. women cannot handle success). In *Taking Stock*, Max Stafford-Clark, the director of the first production of *Top Girls*, recalls attending a reading of the play at the National Theatre in 2000 and taking part in a question-and-answer session afterwards in which this accusation was levelled at him:

> Carole [Hayman: Dull Gret and Angie in the original production of *Top Girls*] says she remembers that I directed the first scene so that it was miserable whereas she says it should be a celebration of women's achievements. Carole is reconstructing history in public according to feminist doctrine. It should be a deft balance

? QUESTION

What does Marlene's inability to define 'success' suggest to you?

of celebration and regret. Celebration, but each of the protagonists has lost children, some of them have been through enormous pain and sacrifice.

(Stafford-Clark and Roberts (2007), p. 211)

 CHECK THE NET

The Last Supper, painted by Leonardo da Vinci, is a famous depiction of the last meal Christ ate with his disciples before going to his death. The painting shows all the disciples seated at a long rectangular table with Christ in the middle. You can see an image of it on the BBC website – go to **www.bbc.co.uk,** search for 'Leonardo' to find the Leonardo homepage, and then click on 'masterpieces' and Last Supper.

The restaurant scene took place at a long table with the seated actors facing the audience, or in profile, rather than with their backs to the audience (too confusing when combined with the overlapping dialogue). Production photographs from the scene recall *The Last Supper* as the guest's engage in animated conversation – some seated, some standing, with Marlene presiding over all in the middle.

The critical response to the play was mostly positive although many critics commented on Lindsay Duncan's unconvincing appearance as Nijo, treating it as a mistake rather than a **Brechtian** device. This may have been the result of their assumptions about plays at the Royal Court Theatre in this period – that they would be political but also **naturalistic** – or perhaps even disapproval about her 'imitating' someone from another culture. Whatever the reason, in Stafford-Clark's revival, Nijo was played by an east Asian actress (Sarah Lam).

THE 1991 PRODUCTIONS

In 1991, Max Stafford-Clark revived the play, for the Royal Court Theatre and a nationwide tour, and with two of the original cast members: Lesley Manville (Griselda in the original production) took the role of Marlene, and Deborah Findlay recreated her roles as Joyce and Isabella Bird. In the intervening period, the play had already begun to earn the status of a modern classic: it had been produced at several major British regional theatres as well as abroad and had become a set text on school and university syllabi in Britain, the USA and Australia. In 1991 it became a set text for the Open University and a version of the play, directed by Stafford-Clark, was filmed for television before the company began performing the stage version. It was broadcast by the BBC which increased the play's audience substantially and further contributed to its place in the **canon** of modern British drama.

The film version began with Act 2, Scene 1, Marlene interviewing Jeanine, in order to establish Marlene as the play's focus. Stafford-Clark thought, and Churchill agreed, that a television audience might find it confusing to be plunged into an **ahistorical** fantasy dinner-party scene. The setting for the dinner party – a large round table (necessary for the camera) in the middle of a cavernous and empty space – did not work as well as Churchill had hoped because the table could be reached only via a grand, curved marble staircase which she felt slowed the action down too much. There was also nothing to indicate the fact that the scene was taking place in a restaurant. In the original production this was achieved by a neon sign; the restaurant was called 'The Prima Donna'; and the waitress was dressed in a 'grecian tunic and sandals' (Robertson, *London Theatre Record* (August–September 1982), p. 470). Marlene was also very friendly to the waitress in this film version, softening her orders with smiles, touching her on the arm, and generally including her in the celebration (none of which is indicated in the text). This adds to the impression of Marlene as a nice person in this scene.

An interesting semiotic difference between this version and the 2002 revival is Shona's appearance (see **Contemporary approaches: Semiotics**). In the 1991 version Shona dressed in jeans, leather jacket and large hooped earrings for her interview with Nell, not the kind of appearance one would expect from a top saleswoman. This raises the intriguing possibility that Nell mistakes her appearance as a sign of her supreme confidence in herself. Or perhaps that she is so taken by Shona's boldness that she gives her the benefit of the doubt until proven otherwise.

By the time the play was revived, the play's themes and pessimism about the future had been proven by the increase in unemployment and widening gulf between the rich and poor, and many critics viewed it as unusually prescient, but also relevant to the climate of the time. As Annalena McAfee, writing in the *Evening Standard* in 1991 put it, 'The intervening decade has given added pertinence to observations about self-gratification and moral responsibility.' For others, the play 'has been badly overtaken by the materialist events of the 1980s which it so accurately forecast and which Churchill went on to document rather more effectively in *Serious Money*' (Morley, *Theatre Record* (April 1991), p. 459).

> **? QUESTION**
>
> What different things could the waitress's appearance and behaviour tell us about the play?

THE 2002 PRODUCTION

By 2002, *Top Girls* was a 'modern classic', but also something of a period piece because of its 1980s references (for example, nuclear war, Maggie and Reagan). Thea Sharrock emphasised the play's historical setting by using 1980s music to introduce each new scene, but chose songs which underscored the play's themes: Madonna's 'Material Girl', Grace Jones's 'Pull Up to the Bumper' and Tina Turner's 'What's Love Got to Do With It?' The songs and the historical setting served to emphasise the relevance of the themes to a modern audience: 'having it all' – combining humanity with ambition and a desire for wealth – still proving as difficult to achieve as in 1982. As Sam Marlowe noted:

> A successful career need not mean remaining childless in the 21st century; but we are still a long way from achieving sexual equality in the workplace, and if Churchill's questions are no longer quite the right ones, they do, at the very least, prompt us to ask others.
>
> (*Theatre Record* (January 2002), p. 40)

The restaurant scene took place at a round table on a revolve (area of the stage which is capable of slowly revolving), allowing the audience to follow who said what to whom, and who seemed to be forging alliances. Griselda's long absence is particularly noticeable in this stage set-up as her empty space continually presents itself to the audience and raises the possibility either that she will not come, or that she will make an astonishing entrance. Of course, she does neither, shuffling apologetically into her seat with the deference we soon learn she is famous for.

www. CHECK THE NET

You can find a review of Sharrock's 2002 production on the British Theatre Guide website – go to **www. britishtheatre guide.info**, click on 'Reviews' and search under 'T'.

PART FOUR

CRITICAL PERSPECTIVES

READING CRITICALLY

This section provides a range of critical viewpoints and perspectives on *Top Girls* and gives a broad overview of key debates, interpretations and theories proposed since the play was published. It is important to bear in mind the variety of interpretations and responses this text has produced, many of them shaped by the critics' own backgrounds and historical contexts.

No single view of the text should be seen as dominant. It is important that you arrive at your own judgements by questioning the perspectives described, and by developing your own critical insights. Objective analysis is a skill achieved through coupling close reading with an informed understanding of the key ideas, related texts and background information relevant to the text. These elements are all crucial in enabling you to assess the interpretations of other readers, and even to view works of criticism as texts in themselves. The ability to read critically will serve you well both in your study of the text, and in any critical writing, presentation or further work you undertake.

CRITICAL RECEPTION AND EARLY REVIEWS

Every time a play is performed it has a different effect on its audience. In some cases this means that critics are baffled about why certain plays were once popular, or, at the other end of the spectrum, why plays which were derided when they were first produced are now considered to be works of genius. This is because plays, like all cultural artefacts, are a product of their time and encapsulate trends and opinions about a variety of different things within their texts and in the moments of their production. For some, *Top Girls* will seem a period piece, a play about the 1980s which has little relevance to life in the twenty-first century (here is a computerless office; there are no mobile phones or emails to bridge the communicative chasm between Joyce and Marlene);

CHECK THE BOOK

Harold Pinter's *The Birthday Party* is a famous example of how audiences react differently to a play. When it was first performed in 1958, the reviews were so bad that it was taken off after a week.

CHECK THE BOOK

London Theatre Record (now *Theatre Record*) compiles reviews of all the major shows in London and the regions from a wide variety of publications. It is published monthly and held by many reference libraries in the UK.

CONTEXT

In the Greek myths the gods are often present on earth disguised as humans in order to meddle in human affairs, produce half-immortal children and cause chaos and disorder in order to revenge themselves on their divine rivals. One of the best known Greek myths is that of Odysseus, who goes wandering across the earth, and returns in disguise to his own home to reassert his claim to his kingdom. There are many different versions of this myth, the most famous being Homer's *The Odyssey.*

CONTEXT

The language used in Francis King's review is, in itself, an indication of the audience he was writing for – educated and theatre literate. 'Inchoate' means not fully formed.

others will see it as timeless because of its focus on family and estranged children and parents (a theme stretching back to the Greek myths).

When the play was first produced, most of the theatre critics on the influential newspapers were men, and, in many cases, they had been in the job for a long time. Because of this they had certain expectations of plays performed at the Royal Court Theatre (political, experimental and **didactic**) and of plays by Caryl Churchill. Many of their reactions could be predicted by the publication they were writing for. For example, Dick Vosburgh wrote a **satirical** sketch as part of his review for *Punch*, which had an older, male and conservative readership – very different to the Royal Court's constituency. Carole Hayman (Dull Gret and Angie in the original production) remembers that, 'the critics were perplexed. The reviews of what has now become a seminal piece – not only of 1980s politics, but also of structural audacity – were, at best, mixed. But audiences loved us and roared every night' (Fitzsimmons (1989), p. 61).

The collected reviews suggest that the critics were not so much perplexed, as divided: most recognised the originality of the play's structure and the formal innovations it made, but not all approved of them. The use of overlapping dialogue was particularly controversial, irksome even, for some of the critics. Francis King of the *Sunday Telegraph* (which also had a conservative readership) suggested 'many of the passages are unintelligible because of the author's directions in the text that they should be spoken simultaneously' and ends his review:

> Max Stafford-Clark has directed an inchoate play, seemingly written on the principle 'I don't know what I think until I get it on to paper' with portentous slowness. Often one waits for the exit line with the same agonised impatience with which one waits for the next bus on a Sunday evening.

In contrast to this, for Michael Coveney of the *Financial Times*, reviewing the play on its return to the Royal Court in 1983: 'overlapping dialogue is a brilliant technical feature of the play'. In an interview for the 1991 production, Stafford-Clark reflected on the peculiar nature of the play's growing success:

> It was not an immediate box-office hit. We then took it to America, to Joseph Papp's Public Theatre, where it was billed as a huge London success and where it played successfully to large audiences. We then returned to the Royal Court with it, where it was billed as a huge American success, and the play was very successful.
>
> (Rabillard (ed.) (1998), p. 76)

(See **Critical approaches: Staging** for more about the first production.)

LATER CRITICISM

In subsequent productions, critics focused on the extent to which the play had predicted the future, in particular the effects of Thatcherism. In an interview given in 1987, Churchill provided an intriguing insight about how the same play can be interpreted in different ways and what this means for the playwright:

> In Greece, for example, where fewer women go out to work, the attitude from some of the men seeing it was, apparently, that the women in the play who'd gone out to work weren't very nice, weren't happy, and they abandoned their children. They felt the play was obviously saying women *shouldn't* go out to work – they took it to mean what they were wanting to say about women themselves, which is depressing … Another example of its being open to misunderstanding was a production in Cologne, Germany, where the women characters were played as miserable and quarrelsome and competitive at dinner, and the women in the office were neurotic and incapable. The waitress slunk about in a catsuit like a bunnygirl and Win changed her clothes on stage in the office. It just turned into a complete travesty of what it was supposed to be. So that's the sort of moment when you think you'd rather write novels, because the productions can't be changed.
>
> (Betsko and Koening (1987), pp. 77–8)

CHECK THE BOOK

See, for example, the reviews of McAfee, Peter, Bayley, Macaulay, Christopher, Asquith and Dodd, collected in *Theatre Record* (9–22 April 1991), which all commented on the accuracy with which *Top Girls* predicted what Britain would become under Thatcherism.

QUESTION

Do you agree with Churchill that it is harder to subvert the authorial intention of a novel or poem?

The questions posed by the play – How can women achieve success in a man's world? What sacrifices are necessary to do so? How can women move forward if they do not stand together? – have remained relevant since the play's first production. In terms of Churchill's **oeuvre**, *Top Girls* comes in the second phase of her career, when her experiments with form had begun, but before she began to work with dance companies and composers, subordinating the **narrative** thrust to physical expression.

CONTEMPORARY APPROACHES

FEMINIST CRITICISM

Feminist criticism has many different objectives: rediscovering the work of 'lost' women writers; re-evaluating the contribution of women to the writings of famous men (for example Wordsworth's sister, Dorothy); assessing the depiction of women in literature; and also exploring the frames of reference within which women discuss their own experiences.

One of the key tenets of the first, second and third waves of the Women's Movement has been the insistence on dividing biological sex (male and female) from gender (male/female). The first is determined by the chemical composition of an individual's DNA – an x and a y chromosome for males, two xs for females; the second is determined by the society in which they are born and raised. In feminist theory, therefore, there is nothing 'essentially' feminine or masculine, they are simply words used in western society to describe traits that are either idealised or assumed to be natural through learned association. Thus, feminist theory allows women to question the idea of 'natural' behaviour: is it 'natural' for women to stay at home and look after the children because they are more feminine than men or is it the result of a number of societal factors – that men historically earn more money than women, that women find it more difficult to return to work immediately after giving birth because of the effects of childbirth on their bodies, and that maternity leave is a relatively recent phenomenon? This questioning of gender assumptions has been key in the development of feminist criticism and also in **queer studies**.

 CHECK THE BOOK

Feminism for Beginners (1992), by Susan Alice Watkins, Marisa Rueda and Marta Rodriguez, is a light-hearted but rigorous exploration of feminism and women's rights explained by cartoons.

Feminists have read *Top Girls* in different ways. For some, the play is a critique of Marlene and her individual ambition and the first act just reinforces the narrowness of her outlook. Lisa Merrill commented that 'by attempting to equate Marlene's promotion at work with the extreme circumstances overcome by the other five guests, Churchill renders Marlene's achievement petty and ludicrous' (see Randall (ed.) (1988), p. 83). For others, this scene represents a collective celebration of women's achievements through the ages and a re-evaluation of women's contribution to history and culture.

Top Girls challenges the definition of what it means to be a successful woman. Many of the women in the play refuse the role of the ideal woman embodied by Griselda: they do not accept their lot as the inevitable consequence of their gender. Although Joyce elected to stay at home and look after Angie, she expresses dissatisfaction with her life, and with her role as a mother: hence her occasional hostility towards Angie. Nell refuses to get married, preferring to maintain her independence and focus on her career; and so does Marlene. In Elaine Aston's words, the women in the play 'refuse the "fixing" of gender roles' and in doing so question the very idea of fixed gender roles (Aston (1997), p. 39).

MARXIST CRITICISM

Marxist criticism focuses on analysing the economic and class basis of texts; in essence, everything comes down to money. It derives from Karl Marx's and Friedrich Engels's analysis and explanation of the infrastructure of capitalism and the construction of the class system – designed to educate the working classes about their oppressed position and encourage them to revolt against it. One of the basic tenets of Marxism is that wealth is the base on which the rest of society (including art and culture) is built. Marxist critical theory (as distinct from political theory) seeks to analyse culture in the light of this knowledge and to challenge critical approaches which assume that a work of art or text is the product of a 'genius' or transcends its socio-economic and cultural circumstances. A Marxist analysis of the Romantic poets, for example, would suggest that the love of nature and solitude celebrated in their poems can be traced to the impact of the Industrial Revolution on rural areas. In

CHECK THE BOOK

Terry Eagleton's *Literary Theory: An Introduction* (1983) provides a clear introduction to Marxist criticism.

CONTEXT

During the Industrial Revolution of the eighteenth century various scientific discoveries moved Britain and Europe from a feudal system (where most people were employed by their local landowner and supplied food and services to the local community) to a mechanised system where the focus was on large-scale production, for example the cloth mills in Manchester and Yorkshire.

CHECK THE BOOK

See Amelia Howe Kritzer's 'Labour and Capital' in her *The Plays of Caryl Churchill* (1991) for an in-depth Marxist reading of the play.

the Lake District, for example, which Wordsworth wrote about extensively, much of the population was encouraged to move to the nearby industrial cities of Lancaster and Manchester to work in the 'dark satanic mills' William Blake criticised. In this reading, then, Wordsworth's poems are not the result of the beauty of the landscape but of an economic imperative.

The focus on work, money and class in *Top Girls* makes it an obvious text for Marxist analysis. Rather than being a 'timeless classic', the play can be seen as a product of its socio-economic time and wrestles with problems peculiar to that time: mass unemployment, the rise of a wealthy meritocracy and the development of a generation of ambitious and avaricious women who will trample over anyone in their determination to achieve success. In this respect it represents the triumph of the individual over the collective and epitomises the capitalist model. Marlene, Win and Nell work in a service industry, and in the 1980s service industries were replacing traditional heavy industry (where the father of Joyce and Marlene worked) as the main source of income and employment (and have continued to do so). This change in the nature of industry helped change the constituency of the workforce and saw an influx of women into the workplace (the hard physical labour involved in most aspects of heavy industry had effectively barred women from entering the labour market in these areas). Women were cheaper to employ because they were doing less skilled jobs, and had less experience of being at work, and therefore commanded lower salaries. It was all a matter of economics.

SEMIOTICS

Semiotics is the study of the way in which signs and sign systems help us make sense of the world. The discipline grew out of linguist Ferdinand de Saussure's attempts to understand how language works as a communicative system. He believed that the relationship between an object, feeling or thought and the word used to describe it is arbitrary (rather than logical) and that this system exists only because of an unspoken agreement to use a particular word (signifier) for a particular thing (signified). In English, for example,

a *dog* is a four-legged canine animal and a *cog* is a small circular
mechanical device and they are distinguished in speech and writing
by their differing initial consonants *d* and *c*. Theorists such as
Claude Levi-Strauss (an anthropologist) and Roland Barthes used
the idea of a system (or structure) to analyse other sign systems used
to create meaning, for example, manners, gesture, dance, advertising,
clothing and, famously in Barthes's case, wrestling. The arbitrary
nature of the relationship between the signifier (be it a word, action
or image) and the signified (meaning) means that there is always the
possibility of the meaning slipping or changing (something often
exploited by advertising).

Semiotics is a useful way of analysing plays, particularly in
performance, because every element of the stage picture has been
carefully chosen to signify something: the set, costumes, body
language and speech of the actors are all choreographed to convey
meaning to the audience. In *Top Girls*, as with all plays, the
costumes and set will contribute to our sense of the individual
characters, particularly in the opening act where the arrival of
Isabella and Nijo dressed in clothes so out of keeping with the
modern dress of Marlene and the decor of the restaurant is the first
indication we get that this is not a **naturalistic** play. Marlene's
clothes will also signal her wealth, in this scene particularly, as she
will be dressed up for the party. In the BBC film of the play the
symbolic significance was increased by the fact that Marlene is
wearing a blue sequined dress. Blue is the colour traditionally
associated with the Conservative Party in Britain, and Margaret
Thatcher often wore blue which served to reinforce the public's
connection between her and the party and to demonstrate her
allegiance to its values. Putting Marlene in a blue dress hints at her
politics and the values she shares with the Prime Minister, while the
sequins signify glamour – as well as wealth – which could be
interpreted as a signal that Marlene has not sacrificed her femininity
in the pursuit of power. The symbolic value of these details is,
however, entirely dependent on the audience's or reader's
knowledge of the cultural significance of blue in this context.
Without this knowledge – this shared understanding of the sign
system – this interpretation falls down.

 **CHECK
THE BOOK**
'Colour Me
Beautiful? Clothes
Consciousness in the
Open University/BBC
Video Production of
Top Girls' by Jane de
Gay in Sheila
Rabillard (ed.)
*Essays on Caryl
Churchill:
Contemporary
Representations*
(1998) discusses the
semiotics of the
costumes in more
detail.

Even without seeing a production of the play, we can make deductions about the semiotics of it. The dress Marlene buys Angie is loaded with significance: for Angie, it is a symbol of her aunt's love and the first step on the road to aping her glamorous lifestyle in the future; for Joyce, it serves as a reminder of Marlene's last visit and the possibility of having Angie taken away from her. The value it has for them explains Joyce's reaction to Angie appearing in it in Act 2, Scene 2 and the reason Angie put it on (memories of Marlene). In this instance it does not matter what the dress looks like, simply that the dress was a gift from Marlene. Its value is **symbolic**.

CHECK THE NET
See **www.fashion-era.com** for images and information on the fashions of the 1980s.

Changes in fashion can also be read semiotically. Fashion in the 1980s embraced extremes: monochrome clothes and fluorescent ones; tight lycra clothes (to show off bodies honed by the craze for aerobics) and billowing ones in floppy expensive fabrics (silk, linen and cashmere). This was the beginning of conspicuous labels on the outside of clothes and bags (logos are another good example of the way symbols work in everyday life). All of these factors communicate information about life in the 1980s: certain sectors of the population had larger disposable incomes to spend on expensive clothes (and, in the case of luxury fabrics such as linen, silk and cashmere, on having them cleaned).

STYLISTICS/LITERARY LINGUISTICS

Stylistics is a discipline that borrows from linguistics and literary criticism in order to offer analyses of the language of texts and, in particular, the way particular effects are achieved through language. It is a particularly useful way of analysing modern plays because it allows comparisons of how 'real' conversation actually works and how conversation in plays is structured in relation to it.

In the case of *Top Girls*, for example, stylistics might analyse the importance of **politeness theory** (who speaks when, who interrupts, who speaks most, the names people call each other) in understanding the power dynamics of the play. Using Paul Grice's conversational maxims, one might analyse whether the appearance of conversational power is supported by the evidence. Grice was a philosopher (rather than a linguist) and formulated the cooperative principle which assumes that people have a shared purpose in conversation and that they operate according to the following unspoken rules:

Quantity – make your contribution as informative as required (but not more or less informative, i.e., too long or too short)
Quality – do not say what you believe to be false (or what you do not have the evidence to support)
Relevance – make your contribution relevant to the current conversations
Manner – make your contribution brief, unambiguous and orderly.

In real life, of course, conversation seldom works on these principles, rather it works on flouting (deliberately breaking) them, and it is in the analysis of flouting that the conversational maxims have become a part of stylistic analysis. As discussed in the **Detailed summaries**, in Act 1, Nijo and Isabella initially dominate the discussion, which reflects their social ease in a formal dining situation. In Act 2, the interviewers control the conversation, reflecting their position of power over their clients. And, in Act 3, Joyce rejects Marlene's attempts to make peace before she has even finished speaking: 'Joyce –', 'No, pet. Sorry' (Act 3, p. 87).

A stylistic or linguistic approach might also investigate **register** (the level of formality of language used by the characters in different situations, and the appropriateness of these choices) and the proximity of their speech to **standard English**. For example, one of the signs of Angie's lack of social awareness is her linguistic behaviour at the Top Girls Agency. Most of the other characters in the play speak more or less as they would write, making sure their speech is grammatical and reasonably formal (apart from swearing). This is particularly true of the characters in Act 2 (the act in which Angie comes to London) because presenting a good image is vital to their job (in the case of the Agency staff) and improves their chances of getting a good job (in the case of the clients). When Angie appears to Marlene she is monosyllabic. She repeats Marlene's questions as replies – 'Are you tired from the journey?', 'Yes, I'm tired from the journey'; and uses 'ungrammatical' speech – 'I just come here. I come to you' (when grammar dictates that she should be speaking in the past tense) (Act 2, p. 54).

CHECK THE BOOK

Exploring the Language of Drama, edited by Jonathan Culpeper, Mick Short and Peter Verdonk (1998), is a collection of accessible essays applying stylistics to dramatic texts (*Cloud Nine* and *The Crucible* among them).

PART FIVE

BACKGROUND

CARYL CHURCHILL'S LIFE AND WORK

In November 1960, Churchill made her first recorded public pronouncement about English drama:

> When *Look Back in Anger* came out it was exciting, but already the working-class intellectual cracking at his wife's caricatured Daddy is a stock character. We know that the English are still snobbish about accents, we're not happy about the British Empire, suburban life is often dull and many middle-aged men are unfulfilled. We can't communicate with each other, have a lot of illusions and don't know what if anything life is about. All right. Where do we go from here?
>
> (*The Twentieth Century*, 168 (November 1960), pp. 443–51)

For Churchill the answer was to be a long career dedicated to pushing the boundaries of traditional English drama: collaborating with actors, musicians, composers, choreographers, directors and other writers in an attempt to explore the problems and preoccupations of contemporary society. The title of the article was, appropriately enough: 'Not Ordinary, Not Safe' – a fitting epithet for a playwright who has consistently shown herself unafraid of conflict and controversy.

 QUESTION

What is 'not ordinary, not safe' about *Top Girls*?

Churchill was born in London in 1938. Her father was a cartoonist, her mother a model. When she was 10, the family moved to Montreal in Canada, and Churchill did not return to England until 1955, just in time to witness the impact made by the English Stage Company at the Royal Court Theatre and the première of Beckett's *Waiting for Godot*. She studied English at Lady Margaret Hall, Oxford, and had several plays produced while she was there: one of them, *Downstairs*, was taken to the newly formed National Student Drama Festival and praised by eminent theatre critic Harold Hobson. After Oxford she married David Harter, a barrister and fellow political activist, and continued to write while bringing up their three children. At this stage of her career she wrote mostly for radio and television, later telling journalists that raising a family meant: 'I could only keep very short images and ideas in my head. Then I had just two or three hours to snatch when I could sit down and work on something.' It was during this period that Churchill became a feminist: 'at first, like most couples, we didn't really question that David was the one who worked'.

Churchill's first professional stage production was *Owners*, produced at the Royal Court Theatre Upstairs in 1972. The play centres on Marion, an ambitious property developer, her inadequate husband, Clegg, whose business is failing in inverse proportion to his wife's success, and her apprentice, Worsley, who is unable to match her merciless approach to tenants, and makes a series of unsuccessful suicide bids during the course of the play. *Owners* prefigures *Top Girls* in several ways: its examination of a successful businesswoman and the personal sacrifices she has made to achieve her position; the issue of adoption; strategies for countering capitalism, and social responsibility. As Churchill explained to one interviewer:

> When I attempt to look at property development in the play from a slightly shifted angle … then I hope we can see this sort of activity for what it is – it becomes a question of whether you think of people … [being] as important as yourself, with feelings, or as objects to be dealt with.

By the time of *Top Girls*, Churchill suggests that people are dangerously close to becoming 'objects to be dealt with', but in *Owners* this manifests itself in Marion's desire for her former lover, Alec, second only to her desire for the building he lives in. The unattainability of both drives her to increasingly desperate measures: she spends so much time at the property that Alec's wife offers her their unborn baby if she will only leave them alone. She accepts, is eventually forced to give the child back, tries to destroy their marriage and orders an arson attack on the house in which Alec dies.

In 1974, Churchill became Royal Court Writer in Residence for a year – the first woman to hold the post. Every interview and piece

CHECK THE NET
There are a number of articles about Churchill and reviews of her plays on the New York Times website. Go to **www.nytimes. com** and search for 'Caryl Churchill'.

of press commentary that covered the event mentioned her age, and the facts that she was married to a barrister and had three children – suggesting that to many people at this time professional women were not seen as separate from their husbands. She wrote two more plays for the Royal Court Theatre Upstairs during this period: *Objections to Sex and Violence* (a middle-class woman's involvement with anarchists) and *Moving Clocks Go Slow* (a 'space play'), as well as two television plays, *Turkish Delight* and *Save it for the Minister*, and a radio play, *Perfect Happiness*. This was also the period in which she began to work collaboratively with companies and individuals – a major change in her working practices after years of researching and writing alone.

CONTEXT

The British director William Gaskill (b. 1930) was formerly artistic director of the Royal Court, Associate Director at the National Theatre and founding member of Joint Stock Theatre Company. Gaskill has been heavily influenced by Brecht and Max Stafford-Clark. He is believed by many to be one of the most rigorous and courageous directors of the post-war period.

Churchill's first collaboration was with Joint Stock, a collective company established by Max Stafford-Clark and William Gaskill whose working method was to hold workshops with writer, director, designer and actors to explore a theme for a play. Sometimes the theme had been determined in advance, and the workshops involved researching themes, trying out improvisations and debating the themes and ideas that informed the play; sometimes the theme emerged during the workshop. Once the initial exploration had been done, the writer wrote the play alone and then returned to the company in order to work on it further. Churchill's first involvement with the group was the project that became *Light Shining in Buckinghamshire* (1976), a play that explored events in England during the Civil War, the many religious and political movements that flourished during the time, and the fact that women were continually excluded from the process. The play incorporated several **Brechtian** devices including an **episodic** structure and the rejection of developed characters (a character was not necessarily played by the same actor every time they appeared – in order to reflect the changing and tumultuous nature of the times).

Churchill's second collaboration was with Monstrous Regiment, a newly formed feminist company, set up to provide more opportunities for female actors (so they do not always have to play a supporting role). Gillian Hanna (one of the founders of the company) recalls that they met Churchill by chance at a political rally in Hyde Park and 'she talked about how in researching her English Civil War play *Light Shining in Buckinghamshire* for Joint Stock, she had come across a mass of material relating to women and witchcraft, and wanted to write a play about it. Her ideas fitted with ours, and we commissioned her to write it' (Hanna (1991), p. xxxvii). The play that resulted from this was *Vinegar Tom*, a good example of a feminist rereading of history. It examines the way in which women were routinely branded as witches for not conforming to society's view of how a woman should speak and behave. This play also incorporated Brechtian elements including song and dance and **ahistorical** interludes which commented on the action. In the introduction to the published play, written in 1982, Churchill comments on her movement from solitary writer to collaborator:

> it was a very enjoyable cooperation with the company. My habit of solitary working had been wiped out by the even greater self-exposure in Joint Stock's method of work. And our shared view of what the play was about and our commitment to it made rewriting precise and easy. ... Though I still wanted to write alone sometimes, my attitude to myself , my work and others had been basically and permanently changed.
>
> (Churchill, *Plays: 1* (1985), p. 131).

From this point on Churchill embarked on a string of collaborative projects, with Joint Stock (*Cloud Nine*, *Fen* and *Serious Money*); with the Central School of Speech and Drama (*Mad Forest*); with choreographer Ian Spink and/or dance company Second Stride (*A Mouthful of Birds*, *Hotel*, *Lives of the Great Poisoners*, *Fugue*, *The Skriker* and *Hotel*); and composer Orlando Gough (who wrote the music for the 1991 revival of *Top Girls* as well as *Lives of the Great Poisoners* and *Hotel*). Between 1991 and 1996 all the work she produced was collaborative, apart from her translation of *Thyestes* for the Royal Court.

Her subsequent plays have continued to explore the moral and social responsibility of individuals in a rapidly changing world through an increasingly pared-down stage picture and text. *Blue*

 CHECK THE BOOK
Rob Ritchie's *The Joint Stock Book: The Making of a Theatre Collective* (1987) has sections on the workshops for *Light Shining in Buckinghamshire*, *Cloud Nine* and *Fen*.

 CHECK THE BOOK
The first volume of Churchill's collected works, *Plays: 1* (1985), has an introduction to *Light Shining in Buckinghamshire*.

CHECK THE NET
The website **www. theatrevoice.com** has several discussions about Churchill's life and work which can be listened to over the web or downloaded. Go to 'Archive' and search for Caryl Churchill.

Heart, also produced at the Royal Court Theatre in 1997, is a double-bill of one-act plays dealing with family ties that moves further from **naturalism**. In *Heart's Desire*, a mother and father wait for their daughter to return from a trip abroad in a scene repeated over and over again. In *Blue Kettle*, a young man preys on vulnerable women who had their children adopted, pretending to be their long-lost son. As the play progresses all the words in their exchanges are replaced by the words 'blue' and 'kettle', further distancing the audience from what is, after all, a perennial dramatic situation: the return of the child thought lost. *Far Away* (2000) posits the idea of a world war so all encompassing that even the animals are taking part; *A Number* (2002) examines the impact of genetics on family and identity; her most recent work, *Drunk Enough to Say I Love You?* (2006), examines the 'special relationship' between the USA and Britain through the conversations of Sam and John who sit on a sofa that rises further and further into the air (and into the blackness) as the action progresses.

Although she is known to dislike interviews and public speaking (preferring her plays to speak for her) Churchill has always been open about her political views, and has voiced her strong convictions in public on a number of occasions: 'I've constantly said that I'm both a socialist and a feminist' (Churchill, unpublished interview). Early on in her career she asked the BBC to remove her name from a production of *Legion Hall Bombings*, an adaptation of the transcript of the trial of William Gallagher in Belfast, in protest at its censorship of the script (as did director Roland Joffe). She challenged *Guardian* columnist Polly Toynbee about her criticism of 'political theatre' and Monstrous Regiment in particular, in a letter to the newspaper in 1979. She also defended Sarah Kane and the Royal Court Theatre against Michael Billington's criticism of the decision to stage *Blasted*. Less publicly she has also objected to the Royal Court's attitude to sponsorship over the years, on one occasion resigning from the Theatre's advisory council over its decision to accept sponsorship from a large bank, and on another stating that she would not write plays for a theatre that took the name of its sponsor.

Churchill's achievements began to be recognised around the time of *Cloud Nine* (winner of an Obie), which began the pattern of her work being produced all over the world. *Top Girls* took the same route but it was really *Serious Money* that brought Churchill international recognition and a degree of financial independence. Ironically, the play's success in London was boosted by the number of city traders who went to see the play, either not realising or caring that their professional and personal ethics were being rigorously critiqued. She is now regarded as one of the world's most influential and experimental playwrights, and, significantly, given her own feminist views, her status as a playwright is no longer regularly qualified by the word 'woman' as it was when *Top Girls* was first written.

CHECK THE BOOK
See Benedict Nightingale's first review of *Top Girls* in *London Theatre Record* (26 August – 8 September 1982).

HISTORICAL BACKGROUND

Churchill was born just before the beginning of the Second World War and moved to Canada when she was 10. This meant that she largely missed the deprivation caused by the war (for example, food rationing), and also grew up without a sense of her place in the class hierarchy. She has frequently commented that on her return to England she was horrified by the lack of equality (across class, gender and race) that she noticed after the liberal atmosphere in Canada. Like many of her generation she was against apartheid, racism, sexism and homophobia.

England in the 1960s was riven with political instability and unrest. In the wake of the post-war consensus which saw the two major political parties in agreement over the main aspects of policy and the establishment of the Welfare State, a rift had emerged. Political opinion was divided over Suez, the Common Market (the 1960s version of the debate about Britain's entry into Europe) and Britain's burgeoning nuclear armoury (the Campaign for Nuclear Disarmament began in 1958). The 1960s also saw the beginning of the liberalisation of sexuality (thanks to the contraceptive pill, the partial decriminalisation of homosexuality and reforms of the divorce and abortion laws) and a period of economic growth and renewed confidence in Britain (helped by the international popularity of the Beatles and other British cultural exports).

CHECK THE BOOK
Andrew Marr's *A History of Modern Britain* (2007) gives a detailed and accessible account of the history of the 1970s and 1980s relevant to *Top Girls*.

CHECK THE BOOK
Jim Cartwright's *Road*, first performed at the Royal Court Theatre in 1986, is set in an unspecified 'road' in northern Britain and examines the effects of unemployment on the local community. The play was written after the Conservative government won its second term in office and when unemployment was heading for 4 million; it offers a much bleaker view of the 1980s than *Top Girls* (written midway through the first term).

The 1970s, by way of comparison, were a time of civil unrest: the beginning of British occupation of Northern Ireland, the miners' strikes, the three-day week (to help cope with fuel shortages) and the deterioration of race relations (as outlined in David Edgar's *Destiny* (1976)).

When Margaret Thatcher came to power in 1979 the trades unions in Britain were believed by many to have more influence over industry than the government did: effectively setting levels of pay and working conditions. They had achieved this power via a series of strikes (when workers would refuse to work until their demands had been met), which culminated in the 'Winter of Discontent' of 1978–9 when the Transport and General Workers' Union (whose members included car manufacturers, haulage drivers, oil tanker drivers, dockers and railway workers) came out on strike, to be followed by public servants, school caretakers, cooks, non-professional hospital workers and Liverpool City Parks and Cemeteries Branch of the General Municipal Workers' Union who refused to bury bodies, or allow others to do it, leading to bodies piling up in cold storage. This strike is one of the iconic moments of the late twentieth century and the memory of the chaos and devastation it caused led many Britons to vote for the Conservative Party for the first time.

Mrs Thatcher was determined to break the power of the unions – indeed she had promised to do so if elected, and she succeeded – thus sounding the death knell for heavy industry in Britain (in a competitive market and without government subsidy British industry could not match the cheaper prices offered by foreign companies). The decline of heavy industry in Britain in the 1980s, which was largely based in the north and west of the country led to talk of a north–south divide. The south of England, particularly London and the counties surrounding it, prospered because of the increase in financial industries located in the City of London, while the traditional manufacturing bases declined, leaving millions of people redundant and living in dilapidated public housing.

Thatcher's Conservative government also determined to revolutionise the socio-economic fabric of Britain by dismantling the Welfare State (a cornerstone of British post-war society hitherto supported by all political parties) in order to free up government money and to create a self-sufficient population. It espoused competitiveness rather than collectivisation and privatised public companies and utilities in a bid to make them more efficient. (Until this point, the telecommunications and transport networks, gas, electricity and water had all been state-owned companies.) Under the Conservatives the nationalised industries were sold off to shareholders, and many ordinary people became shareholders for the first time, buying stakes in British Telecom and British Gas. The Conservatives thought that encouraging people to become shareholders would increase their appetite for stocks and shares and aid the freeing of the money supply. For a discussion of how *Top Girls* reflects the political landscape of the 1980s, see **Themes: Politics**.

LITERARY BACKGROUND

MODERN DRAMA

Churchill has often been described as a cerebral playwright: an oblique reference to the fact that her plays are based on research rather than the observation of human behaviour distilled into a dramatic form (as many **naturalistic** plays are). But she is also a formally innovative one: she was one of the first playwrights to marry **Brecht's** dramatic techniques to political themes, using an **episodic** structure in *Light Shining in Buckinghamshire* and *Serious Money*, incorporating song and commentary into *Vinegar Tom* and *Cloud Nine* and applying a number of other devices outlined in **Critical approaches: Staging**. *Top Girls* has thematic parallels with Brecht's *Mother Courage* (1941) in its exploration and questioning of the choices capitalism forces mothers to make, and comments on the inevitability of history until such time as capitalism implodes.

Yet Churchill also draws on the other major shift in post-war drama: the minimalism of the Absurd. Like Beckett, Churchill has moved towards an increasingly pared-down stage picture and text,

> **CONTEXT**
>
> Theatre of the Absurd is a term coined by critic Martin Esslin to describe theatre which focuses on the absurd position of humans who exist in a world without meaning and where all life is meaningless. Esslin employed the term to describe the work of Beckett, Ionesco and Pinter (among others).

CONTEXT

Among the best known plays of Harold Pinter (b. 1930) are *The Birthday Party* (1957), *The Caretaker* (1959) and *Betrayal* (1978). His overtly political works, e.g. *One for the Road* (1984) and *Mountain Language* (1988), were prompted by the collapse of communism in eastern Europe and the atrocities carried out there.

CONTEXT

In 1956, Ann Jellicoe (b. 1927) won an Observer competition with *The Sport of My Mad Mother*. Her next play, *The Knack* (1962), examined sexual politics in a more startling and original way than *Look Back in Anger*. She wrote and directed several more plays for the Royal Court before setting up the Colway Theatre Trust in 1979.

as if the outward trappings of the play are inversely proportional to the message. Early in her career she told an interviewer that she had stopped writing radio plays because 'I felt this Becketty thing happening: ... I was going to finish up with a play that was two words and a long silence', and her work has sometimes returned to this style, particularly in recent years. Like Pinter, her work has become increasingly and overtly political during the course of her career.

Her growing success, particularly at the Royal Court Theatre during the 1980s, is often tied to the sudden appearance of 'woman playwrights' during this period, and it is certainly true that she contributed greatly to the Court as a theatre receptive to work by women. Between 1959 and 1980 only 8% of the plays produced at the Royal Court were by women, and most of these were by Caryl Churchill and Ann Jellicoe. Yet, as she has pointed out on a number of occasions, she had been writing plays for fourteen years before she had a stage play professionally produced, and she thought of herself as a writer long before it occurred to her to think of herself as a 'woman' writer. She has often told interviewers that her earliest plays were very traditional in form and content, with central male characters examining some 'knotty problem' (quoted in Aston (1997), p. 18). This is not entirely surprising given that her early exposure to theatre and to studying plays at school and university would have comprised traditional male plays of precisely this form. In later plays, she would put these experiences to good use, subverting elements of these forms: for example, the 'reveal' of the **well-made play**; the setting of a dinner to convey information; and the return of the outsider to their family (see **The text: Detailed summaries** for how this is achieved in *Top Girls*).

The influence of women playwrights like Jellicoe and Shelagh Delaney who came to prominence in the 1950s can be detected in Churchill's work. The impact of both Jellicoe's and Delaney's first plays – *The Sport of My Mad Mother* (1956) and *A Taste of Honey* (1958) – has been overshadowed by the Royal Court's most famous product, John Osborne's *Look Back in Anger* (1956). This play concerns the corrosive relationship between Jimmy Porter (a misanthrope) and his wife Alison. The couple live in a bedsit in the

Midlands, and the play opens with Alison Porter wearing one of her husband's shirts while ironing another: one of the most iconic images of post-war drama. For feminists, who in the 1970s began to focus on the unpaid labour women did around the home, this image (and play) **symbolised** a woman's subordination to a man. The furore around the play at the time was prompted by the appearance of the ironing board – seen as marking a new gritty, slice-of-life style of drama.

The plays of Delaney and Jellicoe portrayed a much grittier reality, although not in a naturalistic form. *A Taste of Honey* was set on a council estate in Salford and concerned an unmarried schoolgirl coming to terms with having a mixed-race baby, first with the support of her homosexual friend, Jeff, and then with her alcoholic mother (who sends Jeff away). The **naturalistic** action of the play was disrupted by music from a jazz band (on stage with the actors) and by fantastical scenes within the action. *The Sport of My Mad Mother* followed a female-led gang on the streets of East London and used teenage slang speeded up to create extraordinary speech rhythms. The bizarre nature of the play can be deduced from the Lord Chamberlain's Reader's Report, in which he recommends his superiors to read 'pp.21–22, on which the three characters then on the stage repeat the name "Dolly" eighteen consecutive times before passing onto other topics' (LCP Corr 1957/596). Such experimentation with forms and language can clearly be seen in Churchill's work.

During the 1980s the Royal Court Theatre and other venues staged a growing number of plays by women; this was partly due to the work done by women's theatre groups to raise awareness of women playwrights. Churchill's female contemporaries benefited from this trend. Many of them wrote plays which examined historical, famous and mythical women. As Christopher Innes notes:

History has a particular significance for the feminist movement. As the traditional form of commemorating public events in a society almost exclusively ruled by men, it is seen as promoting a male system of values. Women, relegated to the private sphere, become invisible, reinforcing their subservient status. Just as

---

CONTEXT

Shelagh Delaney's (b. 1939) first play, *A Taste of Honey*, was produced at the Theatre Workshop, Stratford East, in 1958; it transferred to the West End and Broadway and was subsequently made into a film (1961). Her second play, *The Lion in Love* (1960), was not as successful and Delaney renounced theatre in order to write screenplays.

CONTEXT

The Lord Chamberlain, the head of the Royal Household, was responsible for licensing scripts for public performance until 1968. He employed readers to read scripts submitted for production, and report on their suitability to him. The Readers' Reports and scripts are housed at the British Library.

Marxist historians have focussed on the common people, instead of their rulers, so [Pam] Gems asserts that, 'We have our own history to create, to write.'

(Innes (1996), p. 452)

Pam Gems wrote *Piaf* (1978, dramatising the life of French singer Edith Piaf), *Queen Christina* (1977, about the seventeenth-century Swedish queen) and *Camille* (a reworking of Dumas's *Dame aux Camelias*), as well as a number of plays examining the lives of contemporary women (*Loving Women* (1984) is the closest in themes and background to *Top Girls*). Also during this time, Timberlake Wertenbaker wrote *New Anatomies*, a play about Victorian women who dressed as men, for the Women's Theatre Group in 1981 and *The Grace of Mary Traverse* (1985) about women defying conventional roles in the nineteenth century. Most famously, she adapted Thomas Keneally's novel *The Playmaker* to create *Our Country's Good* (1988), a play which examines the redemptive power of theatre on a group of convicts in 1780s Australia.

Sarah Daniels's *Beside Herself* (1990) and Charlotte Keatley's *My Mother Said I Never Should* (1985) both share structural and thematic similarities with *Top Girls*. *Beside Herself* begins with a gathering of biblical women (among them Delilah, Mary Magdalene and Lot's wife) who discuss their lives before dissolving into a scene showing a mother shopping in a supermarket. The play examines the topic of child abuse and the complicity of parents and adults in failing to report it, and the failing mental health support system. *My Mother Said I Never Should* begins with women of different periods playing together as children, emphasising the commonality of their experience before going on to explore the difference in their lifestyles. Churchill's influence can also be seen very clearly in Tony Kushner's *Angels in America, Parts 1 and 2* (1990–2). The play, subtitled 'a gay fantasia on national themes', clearly indicates its non-**naturalistic** political intentions and melds **Brechtian** techniques with biblical imagery, **queer theory** and political commentary.

FICTION AND NON-FICITON

Elaine Aston's *Caryl Churchill* (1997) lists extensive source material for Churchill's plays up to *Lives of the Great Poisoners* (1991). The

CHECK THE FILM
Angels in America was made into a film in 2003, directed by Mike Nicholls and starring Meryl Streep, Emma Thompson and Al Pacino. It won five Golden Globes.

following are some suggestions of works of fiction and non-fiction that also explore the role of women in the modern age.

Virgina Woolf's *A Room of One's Own* (1929) eloquently sets out the competing demands on women writers and the desire for a quiet space in which to work. In the 1930s, Jean Rhys wrote a series of short novels exploring the lives of women seeking to find a way to live with (and without) men: *After Leaving Mr Mackenzie, Voyage in the Dark* and *Good Morning, Midnight*. Doris Lessing's *The Golden Notebook* (1962) is widely regarded as a key feminist tract (although Lessing disputes this). Like Rhys's novels, it chronicles the struggles of a neurotic, clever woman trying to find a way to accommodate her politics and her desire to write with her desire for a meaningful relationship. These conflicting needs are debated at length in the 1970s in two more landmark feminist works: Germaine Greer's *The Female Eunuch* (1970) and Kate Millett's *Sexual Politics* (1971). Both explore the sociological, physiological and financial basis of sexual inequality and urge women to take direct action.

The feminist project of rewriting history produced some brilliantly vivid and enjoyable novels in the 1980s and 1990s, particularly from Angela Carter (1940–92). *Nights at the Circus* (1984) explores the career of Fevvers, a circus aerialiste (high-wire artist) born with wings, and her relationship with American journalist, Jack Walser. Carter mixes comedy, Marxist theory and circus history in a re-imagined Victorian London to explore the subjugation of women. *Wise Children* (1991) surveys the life of twin showgirls, Nora and Dora Chance (a.k.a. the Lucky Chances), the illegitimate offspring of a famous Shakespearean actor. As showgirls, the Chances are always on the seamy side of showbusiness and have plenty of opportunity to observe the exploitation of women, immigrants and the lower classes. Although Carter's novels explore serious subjects they are both witty and touching. A. S. Byatt explores the changing role of women from the 1960s to the 1990s through a series of novels: *The Virgin in the Garden* (1978), *Still Life* (1985) and *Possession* (1990). Margaret Atwood's 1985 novel *The Handmaid's Tale* is a useful companion piece for *Top Girls*. Set at an unspecified point in the future, it envisions a society in which women have been

CHECK THE BOOK
Jean Rhys's *Wide Sargasso Sea* (1966) is a re-examination of Mr Rochester's mad wife Antoinette from *Jane Eyre*, telling the story of their courtship from her point of view, and exploring the dream-like quality of her mental illness.

CHECK THE BOOK
Angela Carter's *The Bloody Chamber* (1979) is a collection of fairy tales re-told from the perspective of the female characters; it includes versions of Little Red Riding Hood, Beauty and the Beast and Bluebeard.

CHECK THE FILM

The Handmaid's Tale was made into a film in 1990, adapted by Harold Pinter, starring Natasha Richardson, Robert Duvall and Faye Dunaway.

co-opted as birth-mothers for the ruling class. They have been reduced to their essential biological function and made subservient handmaidens (in the same way as Griselda is a kind of handmaiden to her husband) with no autonomy.

World events	Author's life	Literary events
1938 German occupation of Austria	**1938** (2 September) Born in London	
1939 Spanish Civil War ends; Second World War begins when Germany invades Poland		**1939** Noel Coward, *This Happy Breed*; T. S. Eliot, *The Family Reunion*; Jean Rhys, *Good Morning, Midnight*
1940 Winston Churchill (Conservative) elected British Prime Minister		**1940** Bertolt Brecht, *Mother Courage and Her Children*; Graham Greene, *The Power and the Glory*
1941 Japan attacks American naval base Pearl Harbour, Hawaii; USA joins Second World War in Europe and the Pacific		**1941** Coward, *Blithe Spirit*; Eliot, *The Dry Salvages*
1944 Butler Education Act makes education up to the age of 15 compulsory for all British children		**1944** Joyce Carey, *The Horse's Mouth*
1945 End of Second World War in Europe and the Pacific (atomic bombs dropped on Hiroshima and Nagasaki); Clement Atlee (Labour) elected British Prime Minister and nationalises major industries		**1945** George Orwell, *Animal Farm*; Evelyn Waugh, *Brideshead Revisited*
1946 National Health Service established in Britain		**1946** Philip Larkin, *Jill*; J. B. Priestley, *An Inspector Calls*
1947 Britain grants India independence		**1947** Anne Frank, *The Diary of a Young Girl*; Tennessee Williams, *A Streetcar Named Desire*
1948 Jewish state of Israel established	**1948** Churchill moves to Montreal, Canada, with her family; attends Trafalgar School until 1955	

World events	Author's life	Literary events
		1949 Simone De Beauvoir, *The Second Sex*; Eliot, *The Cocktail Party*; Arthur Miller, *Death of a Salesman*; Orwell, *Nineteen Eighty-four*
1950–3 Korean War		**1950** G. B. Shaw dies; Samuel Beckett, *Molloy*
1951 Winston Churchill re-elected British Prime Minister; Festival of Britain		**1951** Anthony Powell, *A Question of Upbringing*
1952 Accession of Queen Elizabeth II to throne of Britain		**1952** Che Guevara, *The Motorcycle Diaries*
1954 End of food rationing in Britain; first hydrogen bomb exploded		**1954** Kingsley Amis, *Lucky Jim*; William Golding, *Lord of the Flies*; Terence Rattigan, *Separate Tables*; J. R. R. Tolkien, *The Fellowship of the Ring*
	1955 Leaves Montreal	**1955** Beckett, *Waiting for Godot*; first English production of Bertolt Brecht's *Mother Courage*; National Student Drama Festival established
1956 Suez Crisis; Russia invades Hungary		**1956** Brecht dies; John Osborne, *Look Back in Anger*
1957 In Britain, Wolfenden Report on Homosexual Offences and Prostitution recommends the decriminalisation of homosexual acts between men over the age of 21	**1957** Begins studying English Literature and Language at Lady Margaret Hall, Oxford	**1957** Beckett, *Endgame*; Osborne, *The Entertainer*; Stevie Smith, 'Not Waving But Drowning'
1958 Campaign for Nuclear Disarmament established in Britain – first Aldermaston March	**1958** Student production of *Downstairs*, staged by Oriel College Dramatic Society, subsequently taken to National Student Drama Festival in 1959	**1958** Chinua Achebe, *Things Fall Apart*; Brendan Behan, *The Hostage*; Shelagh Delaney, *A Taste of Honey*; Ann Jellicoe, *The Sport of My Mad Mother*; Harold Pinter, *The Birthday Party*

World events	Author's life	Literary events
1960 Britain grants Ghana independence	**1960** Graduates from Oxford; writes *Easy Death*; a student production of *Having a Wonderful Time*; contributes article to journal *Twentieth Century*, 'Not Ordinary, Not Safe: A Direction for Drama?'	**1960** D. H. Lawrence's *Lady Chatterley's Lover* (previously banned under the Obscene Publications Act of 1920) decreed not to be obscene and published by Penguin
1961 USA invades Cuba; major CND demonstration in Britain; Berlin Wall built	**1961** Writes *The Ants*; marries David Harter; student productions of *Easy Death* and *You've No Need to be Frightened*	**1961** Beckett *Happy Days*; Thom Gunn, *My Sad Captains*; Jellicoe, *The Knack*; Waugh, *Sword of Honour*
1962 Cuban Missile Crisis	**1962** *The Ants*, first professional radio play, produced for BBC	**1962** Anthony Burgess, *A Clockwork Orange*; Doris Lessing, *The Golden Notebook*
1963 US President Kennedy assassinated	**1963** First child, Joe Harter, born	**1963** Sylvia Plath, *The Bell Jar*; Muriel Spark, *The Girls of Slender Means*; Theatre Workshop, *Oh! What a Lovely War*
1964 Harold Wilson (Labour) elected British Prime Minister	**1964** Paul Harter born	**1964** Larkin, *The Whitsun Weddings*; Joe Orton, *Entertaining Mr Sloane*
1965 US bombing of Vietnam begins; abolition of capital punishment in Britain	**1965** Writes *Lovesick*	**1965** Edward Bond's *Saved* and Osborne's *A Patriot for Me* challenge Lord Chamberlain's power to pre-censor plays; Pinter, *The Homecoming*; Plath, *Ariel*
1966 In Britain, abortion legalised; Sexual Offences Act legalises homosexuality	**1966** *Lovesick* broadcast on BBC radio	**1966** Jean Rhys, *Wide Sargasso Sea*
1968 Russian invades Czechoslovakia; Theatres Act repeals Lord Chamberlain's powers to censor drama in Britain; women's strike at Ford factory in Dagenham brings production to a halt	**1968** Writes *The Marriage of Toby's Idea of Angela and Angela's Idea of Toby*; *Identical Twins* broadcast on BBC radio	

World events

1969 British troops go into Northern Ireland; Divorce Reform Act in Britain allows a couple to divorce by mutual consent after being separated for two years; Equal Pay rally in Trafalgar Square

1970 Edward Heath (Conservative) becomes British Prime Minister; Women's Liberation Movement founded in Britain; first national Women's Liberation Conference held at Ruskin College; Gay Liberation Front founded

1971 National Women's Liberation March in Britain

1972 Direct rule of Northern Ireland begins; miners' strike in Britain; *Spare Rib* (monthly feminist magazine) and *Gay News* founded

1973 Britain joins the EEC; fuel shortages lead to a three-day working week in Britain

Author's life

1969 Rick Harter born

1971 Writes *Henry's Past* and *The Judge's Wife; Abortive* and *Not...not...not...not...not enough oxygen* broadcast on BBC radio

1972 Writes *The Hospital at the Time of the Revolution*; radio plays *Schreber's Nervous Illness* and *Henry's Past* broadcast on BBC; *The Judge's Wife* televised on BBC; *Owners* at Royal Court Theatre Upstairs

1973 Writes *Moving Clocks Go Slow, Turkish Delight* and *Perfect Happiness*; *Perfect Happiness* broadcast on BBC radio; *Owners* staged at Mercer Shaw Theatre, New York

Literary events

1969 Orton, *What the Butler Saw*; David Storey, *In Celebration*

1970 Germaine Greer, *The Female Eunuch*; Ted Hughes, *Crow*; Women's Street Theatre and Gay Street Theatre Groups protest against Miss World contest being held at Albert Hall

1971 Kate Millett, *Sexual Politics*

1972 Red Ladder's *A Woman's Work is Never Done*; Women's Street Theatre Group, *Equal Pay Show*

1973 Women's Theatre Festival at the Almost Free Theatre

World events

1974 Harold Wilson (Labour) re-elected British Prime Minister; second miners' strike

1975 Margaret Thatcher elected leader of Conservative Party in Britain

1977 Grunwick Print disputes; 1.3 million unemployed in Britain

1978 Saatchi & Saatchi run Conservative Party's advertising campaign ('Labour Isn't Working')

1979 In Britain, Winter of Discontent – mass strikes; Margaret Thatcher (Conservative) elected British Prime Minister; Soviet Union invades Afghanistan

Author's life

1974 Appointed resident dramatist at Royal Court for a year – first woman to hold post; writes *Objections to Sex and Violence*; *Turkish Delight* televised on BBC

1975 *Perfect Happiness* produced at the Soho Poly; *Objections to Sex and Violence* and *Moving Clocks Go Slow* produced at Royal Court

1976 Writes *Traps*; *Light Shining in Buckinghamshire* (first collaboration with Joint Stock Theatre Group and Max Stafford-Clark) and *Vinegar Tom* (collaboration with Monstrous Regiment Theatre Company) staged at Royal Court and Humberside Theatre, Hull, respectively

1977 Contributes to Monstrous Regiment's feminist cabaret *Floorshow*; *Traps* produced at the Royal Court Upstairs

1978 BBC televises *After Dinner Joke* and *Legion Hall Bombing*; writes *Softcops*

1979 *Cloud Nine* produced at Royal Court

Literary events

1974 Women's Theatre Group and Women's Theatre Company founded; Women's Theatre Company stages Pam Gems's *Go West Young Woman*

1975 Women's theatre company Monstrous Regiment founded; Seamus Heaney, *North*

1976 David Edgar, *Destiny*

1977 Virago Press founded; Gems, *Queen Christina* and *Dusa, Fish, Stas and Vi*

1978 Women's Press founded; Gems, *Piaf*; Bryony Lavery, *Time Gentlemen Please*; Michelene Wandor, *Whores D'Oeuvres*

1979 Martin Sherman, *Bent*

World events

1980 Ronald Reagan (Republican) elected President of the USA; hunger strikes at Maze Prison, Northern Ireland; unemployment in Britain at 2.7 million

1981 Urban riots in Liverpool, Manchester, Brixton and Southall (London); second hunger strike at Maze Prison; Women's Peace Camp set up at Greenham Common

1982 Britain goes to war with Argentina over the Falkland Islands

1983 Thatcher re-elected as British Prime Minister

1984 Reagan re-elected President of the USA; third miners' strike in Britain

1985 Miners' strike ends in Britain

Author's life

1980 Begins *Top Girls*; tutors Royal Court Young Writers Group; *Three More Sleepless Nights* produced at Soho Poly; *Cloud Nine* revived at Royal Court

1981 Writes *Crimes*; *Cloud Nine* has US and Australian premières

1982 *Crimes* televised by BBC; *Top Girls* produced at Royal Court, directed by Max Stafford-Clark, transfers to New York; *Cloud Nine* wins an Obie, premières in New Zealand, Japan, Denmark, West Germany and Belgium

1983 *Fen* produced at the Almeida Theatre, then Royal Court, then New York; *Top Girls* returns to Royal Court and premières in Australia, Sweden, Japan, West Germany, Greece and Switzerland

1984 *Softcops*, Barbican Pit; contributes to *Midday Sun*, performed at the ICA; wins Susan Smith Blackburn Award for *Fen*; *Top Girls* premières in Denmark, Norway, New Zealand and Yugoslavia

Literary events

1980 Howard Brenton, *The Romans in Britain*; Andrea Dunbar, *The Arbor*; Willy Russell, *Educating Rita*

1981 Salman Rushdie, *Midnight's Children*

1982 Alice Walker, *The Color Purple*

1983 Sarah Daniels, *Masterpieces*; Edgar, *Maydays*; David Mamet, *Glengarry Glen Ross*

1984 Angela Carter, *Nights at the Circus*; Gems, *Camille* and *Loving Women*; Jeanette Winterson, *Oranges are not the Only Fruit*

1985 Margaret Atwood, *The Handmaid's Tale*; Benjamin Zephaniah, *Dread Affair*

World events	Author's life	Literary events
	1986 *A Mouthful of Birds* by Churchill and David Lan; writes *Serious Money*; *Cloud Nine* premières in Austria; *Top Girls* in Iceland and Austria	**1986** Jim Cartwright, *Road*; Russell, *Shirley Valentine*
	1987 *Serious Money*, Royal Court Theatre; *Fugue* (written with Ian Spink) televised by BBC	**1987** Charlotte Keatley, *My Mother Said I Never Should*
1988 George Bush elected President of the USA; 'Black Monday' (financial crash) sends Britain into recession	**1988** *Serious Money* premières in New York	**1988** Tony Harrison, *V*; Timberlake Wertenbaker, *Our Country's Good*
1989 Fall of Berlin Wall marks the collapse of communism in eastern Europe	**1989** *Icecream* and *Hot Fudge* staged at Royal Court; Churchill resigns from Council of the English Stage Company over sponsorship	**1989** Alan Ayckbourn, *Revenger's Comedies*
1990 Paris summit ends Cold War; Poll Tax riots in Britain; Thatcher resigns as Prime Minister and is replaced by John Major	**1990** Travels to Romania with students from Central School of Speech and Drama; writes *Mad Forest: A Play from Romania* about revolution of 1989	**1990** Eavan Boland, *Outside History*; A. S. Byatt, *Possession*; Tony Kushner, *Angels in America*, Part 1
1991 First Gulf War; IRA bombs Downing Street	**1991** *Lives of the Great Poisoners* produced; Stafford-Clark revives *Top Girls* at Royal Court and directs a version for BBC television; *Top Girls* is put on Open University syllabus	**1991** Carter, *Wise Children*
1992 Conservatives re-elected under Major; 'Black Wednesday' – Britain plunged into economic crisis		**1992** Kushner, *Angels in America*, Part 2
		1993 Irvine Welsh, *Trainspotting*

World events	Author's life	Literary events
	1994 Translation of *Thyestes* staged at Royal Court Theatre Upstairs; *The Skriker* staged at the National Theatre	**1994** Boland, *In a Time of Violence*
		1995 Edgar, *Pentecost*; Sarah Kane, *Blasted*
		1996 Roddy Doyle, *The Woman Who Walked into Doors*; Helen Fielding, *Bridget Jones's Diary*
1997 Tony Blair (Labour) elected Prime Minister of Britain	**1997** *Hotel* performed by Second Stride at the Place, London; *This is a Chair* staged at Royal Court; *Blue Heart* directed by Stafford-Clark	**1997** Toni Morrison, *Paradise*
1998 Good Friday Agreement in Northern Ireland	**1998** Churchill objects to proposals to rename Royal Court after its sponsors	
	1999 *This is a Chair* produced Royal Court Upstairs	
	2000 *Far Away* produced at Royal Court	
2001 Terrorist attacks on New York and Washington		**2001** Zephaniah, *Too Black, Too Strong*
	2002 *A Number* produced at Royal Court; *Top Girls* revived at Aldwych Theatre, London	
2003 Britain and USA declare war on Iraq		
	2006 *Drunk Enough to Say I Love You?* produced at Royal Court	

OTHER WORKS BY CARYL CHURCHILL

Owners, in *Plays: 1*, Methuen, 1985

Cloud Nine, in *Plays: 1*, Methuen, 1985

Serious Money, in *Plays: 2*, Methuen, 1990

Blue Heart, Nick Hern Books, 1997

See also:

Vinegar Tom, in *Plays: 1*, Methuen, 1985

Mad Forest in *Plays: 3*, Nick Hern Books, 2001

A Number, Nick Hern Books, 2002

Plays: 1, Methuen, 1985
   includes *Owners, Traps, Vinegar Tom, Light Shining in Buckinghamshire, Cloud Nine*

Plays: 2, Methuen, 1990
   includes *Softcops, Top Girls, Fen, Serious Money*

Plays: 3, Nick Hern Books, 2001
   includes *Icecream, Mad Forest, Thyestes, The Skriker, A Mouthful of Birds, Lives of the Great Poisoners*

Churchill Shorts, Nick Hern Books, 1990
   includes *Three More Sleepless Nights, Lovesick, The After-dinner Joke, Abortive, Schreber's Nervous Illness, The Judge's Wife, The Hospital at the Time of the Revolution, Hot Fudge, Not... Not... Not... Not... Not Enough Oxygen, Seagulls*

WIDER READING

For connections and comparisons with *Top Girls* see the relevant pages of these Notes (provided in bold below):

MODERN DRAMA
Jim Cartwright, *Road*, 1986 **(p. 96)**

Sarah Daniels, *Beside Herself*, 1990 **(p. 100)**

Shelagh Delaney, *A Taste of Honey*, 1958 **(pp. 98–9)**

Andrea Dunbar, *The Arbor*, 1980 **(p. 44)**

Pam Gems, *Queen Christina*, 1977 **(p. 100)**

Ann Jellicoe, *The Sport of My Mad Mother*, 1958 **(pp. 98–9)**

Sarah Kane, *Blasted*, 1995 **(p. 94)**

Charlotte Keatley, *My Mother Said I Never Should*, 1987 **(pp. 28, 56, 100)**

Tony Kushner, *Angels in America, Parts 1 and 2*, 1990–2 **(p. 100)**

David Mamet, *Glengarry Glen Ross*, 1983 **(p. 31)**

Harold Pinter, *The Homecoming*, 1965 **(p. 37)**

Willy Russell, *Educating Rita*, 1980 **(p. 43)**

David Storey, *In Celebration*, 1969 **(p. 39)**

Timberlake Wertenbaker, *Our Country's Good*, 1988 **(p. 100)**

MODERN PROSE FICTION
Margaret Atwood, *The Handmaid's Tale*, 1985 **(p. 101)**

——, *The Penelopiad*, 2005, **(p. 9)**

A. S. Byatt, *Possession*, 1990 **(p. 101)**

Angela Carter, *Nights at the Circus*, 1984 **(p. 101)**

——, *Wise Children*, 1991 **(p. 101)**

Michael Frayn, *Spies*, 2002 **(p. 34)**

Jean Rhys, *Voyage in the Dark*, 1934 **(p. 101)**

——, *Good Morning, Midnight*, 1939 **(p. 101)**

——, *Wide Sargasso Sea*, 1966 **(p. 101)**

MODERN PROSE NON-FICTION
Judith Butcher, *Gender Trouble*, 1990 **(p. 18)**

Germaine Greer, *The Female Eunuch*, 1970 **(p. 101)**

Kate Millett, *Sexual Politics*, 1971 **(p. 101)**

MODERN POETRY
Maya Angelou, *And Still I Rise*, 1978 **(p. 55)**

Carol Ann Duffy, *The World's Wife*, 1999 **(p. 60)**

LITERARY CRITICISM

Elaine Aston, *Caryl Churchill* [1997], 2nd edn, Northcote Press, 2000
A book-length study of Churchill's plays, from her early work for radio up to *Far Away*; contains a detailed biographical outline

Elaine Aston and Janelle Reinelt, *The Cambridge Companion to Modern British Women Playwrights*, Cambridge University Press, 2000
Contains the essay by Janelle Reinelt, 'Caryl Churchill and the Politics of Style'

Kathleen Betsko and Rachel Koenig (eds), *Interviews with Contemporary Women Playwrights*, Beech Tree Books, 1987

Geraldine Cousin, *Churchill the Playwright*, Methuen, 1989

Richard Eyre and Nicholas Wright, *Changing Stages: A View of British Theatre in the Twentieth Century*, Bloomsbury, 2000
Divided thematically rather than chronologically, this is a valuable survey compiled by directors rather than academics

Linda Fitzsimmons, *File on Churchill*, Methuen, 1989
An extremely useful reference work outlining all of Churchill's plays (up to *Fugue*), and reproducing reviews and other criticism, particularly good on details of her earliest works

Frances Gray (ed.), *Second Wave Plays: Women at the Albany Empire*, Sheffield Academic Press, 1990

Gillian Hanna, *Monstrous Regiment: A Collective Celebration*, Nick Hern Books, 1991
Contains four of the plays it performed and a history of the company

Christopher Innes, *Modern British Drama* [1996], rev. edn, Cambridge University Press, 2000
Contains the chapter 'Caryl Churchill: From the Psychology of Feminism to the Surreal'

Amelia Howe Kritzer, *The Plays of Caryl Churchill*, Macmillan, 1991
A critical work which analyses Churchill's work thematically. *Top Girls* is discussed in Chapter 7, 'Labour and Capital'

Ruth Little and Emily McLaughlin, *The Royal Court: Inside Out*, Oberon Books, 2007
A history of the theatre drawn from the theatre's archives and the memories of those who worked there

Sheridan Morley, *Shooting Stars: Plays and Players 1975–1983*, Quartet, 1983

Sheila Rabillard (ed.), *Essays on Caryl Churchill: Contemporary Representations*, Blizzard Publishing, 1998
Contains three chapters on *Top Girls*, two of which analyse the BBC film version

Phyllis Randall (ed.), *Caryl Churchill: A Casebook*, Garland, 1988

Rob Ritchie, *The Joint Stock Book: The Making of a Theatre Collective*, Methuen, 1987

Bryan Robertson, *Spectator*, reprinted in *London Theatre Record*, 26 August–8 September 1982, p. 470

Elaine Showalter, *A Literature of Their Own: British Women Novelists from Brontë to Lessing*, rev. edn, Virago, 1982
Useful for background and wider reading

——, *The New Feminist Criticism: Essays on Women, Literature, and Theory*, Virago, 1986

Max Stafford-Clark and Philip Roberts, *Taking Stock: The Theatre of Max Stafford-Clark*, Nick Hern Books, 2007
Discusses the development of *Cloud Nine* and *Serious Money*

Michelene Wandor, *Carry On, Understudies: Theatre and Sexual Politics*, Routledge, 1986

——, *Look Back in Gender: Sexuality and the Family in Post-war British Drama*, Methuen, 1987

FILMS

The National Video Archive of Performance has filmed the 2007 revival of *Cloud Nine* at the Almeida Theatre, *Far Away* at the Royal Court Upstairs in 2000 and the 2002 revival of *Top Girls* at the Aldwych Theatre. These are all available to view on request from the V&A Theatre Collections

The Open University/BBC film of *Top Girls* complete with interviews and commentary is available from Routledge

LITERARY TERMS

ahistorical not following a historical or chronological structure; outside history

Brechtian the methods or style of theatre pioneered by German playwright and director Bertolt Brecht: among them the deployment of alienation techniques to distance the audience from the action on stage to give it opportunity to analyse what is happening and why

canon in literary critical terms, a body of work thought to represent the best of its type, or the most widely studied. In the late twentieth century, the study of literature has moved away from studying the 'canon' and has embraced a wider range of literature

counterpoint the juxtaposition of one theme, style or voice with another to give texture and depth to a literary or musical work

dialect a variety of speech, usually associated with geographical location, rather than social status; dialect covers vocabulary and syntax, accent covers the sound of the speech

dialogue literally, speech exchanges between two people; used in drama to refer to the speech exchanges between any number of characters

didactic work of art or literature meant to instruct

episodic in short sections, without a through **narrative**

euphemism a veiled expression or word used to avoid a taboo phrase or concept, for example 'passed on' for 'died'

farce style of comic drama in which coincidences and unfortunate events escalate to the point of chaos

homily a sermon, or moralising discourse

imagery descriptive language which uses images to make actions, objects and characters more vivid in the reader's mind; **metaphors** and **similes** are examples of imagery

irony/ironic words or situation in which the intended effect is opposite to the literal meaning of the words or actual effect

loquacious talkative

metaphor a figure of speech in which a word or phrase is applied to an object, a character or an action which does not literally belong to it, in order to imply a resemblance and create an unusual or striking image in the reader's mind

motif theme, image or reference which recurs throughout a work of literature or piece of music

narrative a story of happenings or events

naturalist/naturalism literary genre which seeks to reflect real life as truthfully as possible, both in terms of language and in the setting of the work; often used interchangeably with **realism**

oeuvre a body of work

pathos the power of arousing feelings of pity and sorrow in a work

patriarchy a system of society or government ruled by men and organised for the convenience of men

politeness theory a branch of linguistics which looks at how people speak to each other to reveal information, for example about their relative social status and intentions

queer studies strand of cultural/critical theory which challenges society's assumptions about gender and sexuality as fixed and unchangeable and argues instead that there is nothing 'innate' about gender or sexuality

realism see **naturalism**

register a variety of language, most often used to refer to variations in the formality of speech depending on the relationship of the addresser and the addressee; for example, one might speak in an informal register to a friend, but in a formal one to one's doctor

Restoration comedy a play written after the restoration of the monarchy in 1660, mocking social conventions and manners, and celebrating sexual desire and cunning

satire a type of literature in which folly, evil or topical issues are held up to scorn through ridicule, irony or exaggeration

simile a figure of speech which compares two things using the words 'like' or 'as'

standard English the variety of the English spoken language with the most prestige, and which is closest to the written form of English; the spoken form is usually associated with higher social classes and educated discourses

sub-text/sub-textual literally beneath the surface of the text; usually refers to information not openly conveyed by the text but commonly understood by readers and audiences

symbolism investing material objects with abstract powers and meanings greater than their own; allowing a complex idea to be represented by a single object

well-made play a dramatic form developed in the nineteenth century and used for most social dramas and comedies of the Victorian period, it has a clear structure and a tidy resolution in which the good are rewarded and the bad (or morally dubious) are punished; usually begins with an exposition which tells the audience what it needs to know (e.g. that someone has a secret), followed by development and complication (actions which bring the play to a crisis point) and then resolution

Kate Dorney has a BA in English Language and Literature from the University of Oxford, an MA in Twentieth-century Studies from King's College London and a PhD in drama and linguistics from the University of Sheffield. She is the Curator of Modern and Contemporary Performance at the V&A Theatre Collections, a department of the Victoria and Albert Museum. She has written widely on post-war British theatre including works on playwrights Joe Orton and Samuel Beckett and actor Ralph Richardson.

GCSE

Maya Angelou
I Know Why the Caged Bird Sings

Jane Austen
Pride and Prejudice

Alan Ayckbourn
Absent Friends

Elizabeth Barrett Browning
Selected Poems

Robert Bolt
A Man for All Seasons

Harold Brighouse
Hobson's Choice

Charlotte Brontë
Jane Eyre

Emily Brontë
Wuthering Heights

Brian Clark
Whose Life is it Anyway?

Robert Cormier
Heroes

Shelagh Delaney
A Taste of Honey

Charles Dickens
David Copperfield
Great Expectations
Hard Times
Oliver Twist
Selected Stories

Roddy Doyle
Paddy Clarke Ha Ha Ha

George Eliot
Silas Marner
The Mill on the Floss

Anne Frank
The Diary of a Young Girl

William Golding
Lord of the Flies

Oliver Goldsmith
She Stoops to Conquer

Willis Hall
The Long and the Short and the Tall

Thomas Hardy
Far from the Madding Crowd
The Mayor of Casterbridge
Tess of the d'Urbervilles
The Withered Arm and other Wessex Tales

L. P. Hartley
The Go-Between

Seamus Heaney
Selected Poems

Susan Hill
I'm the King of the Castle

Barry Hines
A Kestrel for a Knave

Louise Lawrence
Children of the Dust

Harper Lee
To Kill a Mockingbird

Laurie Lee
Cider with Rosie

Arthur Miller
The Crucible
A View from the Bridge

Robert O'Brien
Z for Zachariah

Frank O'Connor
My Oedipus Complex and Other Stories

George Orwell
Animal Farm

J. B. Priestley
An Inspector Calls
When We Are Married

Willy Russell
Educating Rita
Our Day Out

J. D. Salinger
The Catcher in the Rye

William Shakespeare
Henry IV Part I
Henry V
Julius Caesar
Macbeth
The Merchant of Venice
A Midsummer Night's Dream
Much Ado About Nothing
Romeo and Juliet
The Tempest
Twelfth Night

George Bernard Shaw
Pygmalion

Mary Shelley
Frankenstein

R. C. Sherriff
Journey's End

Rukshana Smith
Salt on the Snow

John Steinbeck
Of Mice and Men

Robert Louis Stevenson
Dr Jekyll and Mr Hyde

Jonathan Swift
Gulliver's Travels

Robert Swindells
Daz 4 Zoe

Mildred D. Taylor
Roll of Thunder, Hear My Cry

Mark Twain
Huckleberry Finn

James Watson
Talking in Whispers

Edith Wharton
Ethan Frome

William Wordsworth
Selected Poems

A Choice of Poets

Mystery Stories of the Nineteenth Century including The Signalman

Nineteenth Century Short Stories

Poetry of the First World War

Six Women Poets

For the AQA Anthology:

Duffy and Armitage & Pre-1914 Poetry

Heaney and Clarke & Pre-1914 Poetry

Poems from Different Cultures

Key Stage 3

William Shakespeare
Henry V
Macbeth
Much Ado About Nothing
Richard III
The Tempest